LISP 1.5 Programmer's Manual

The Computation Center
and Research Laboratory of Electronics

Massachusetts Institute of Technology

John McCarthy
Paul W. Abrahams
Daniel J. Edwards
Timothy P. Hart
Michael I. Levin

The M. I. T. Press
Massachusetts Institute of Technology
Cambridge, Massachusetts

The Research Laboratory of Electronics is an interdepartmental laboratory in which faculty members and graduate students from numerous academic departments conduct research.

The research reported in this document was made possible in part by support extended the Massachusetts Institute of Technology, Research Laboratory of Electronics, jointly by the U.S. Army, the U.S. Navy (Office of Naval Research), and the U.S. Air Force (Office of Scientific Research) under Contract DA36-039-sc-78108, Department of the Army Task 3-99-25-001-08; and in part by Contract DA-SIG-36-039-61-G14; additional support was received from the National Science Foundation (Grant G-16526) and the National Institutes of Health (Grant MH-04737-02).

Reproduction in whole or in part is permitted for any purpose of the United States Government.

SECOND EDITION

ISBN-13 978-0-262-13011-0 (paperback)

PREFACE

The over-all design of the LISP Programming System is the work of John McCarthy and is based on his paper "Recursive Functions of Symbolic Expressions and Their Computation by Machine" which was published in <u>Communications</u> <u>of</u> <u>the</u> <u>ACM</u>, April 1960.

This manual was written by Michael I. Levin.

The interpreter was programmed by Stephen B. Russell and Daniel J. Edwards.

The print and read programs were written by John McCarthy, Klim Maling, Daniel J. Edwards, and Paul W. Abrahams.

The garbage collector and arithmetic features were written by Daniel J. Edwards.

The compiler and assembler were written by Timothy P. Hart and Michael I. Levin. An earlier compiler was written by Robert Brayton.

The "LISP 1 Programmer's Manual," March 1, 1960, was written by Phyllis A. Fox.

Additional programs and suggestions were contributed by the following members of the Artificial Intelligence Group of the Research Laboratory of Electronics: Marvin L. Minsky, Bertram Raphael, Louis Hodes, David M. R. Park, David C. Luckham, Daniel G. Bobrow, James R. Slagle, and Nathaniel Rochester.

August 17, 1962

TABLE OF CONTENTS

CONTENTS

I. THE LISP LANGUAGE

The LISP language is designed primarily for symbolic data processing. It has been used for symbolic calculations in differential and integral calculus, electrical circuit theory, mathematical logic, game playing, and other fields of artificial intelligence.

LISP is a formal mathematical language. It is therefore possible to give a concise yet complete description of it. Such is the purpose of this first section of the manual. Other sections will describe ways of using LISP to advantage and will explain extensions of the language which make it a convenient programming system.

LISP differs from most programming languages in three important ways. The first way is in the nature of the data. In the LISP language, all data are in the form of symbolic expressions usually referred to as S-expressions. S-expressions are of indefinite length and have a branching tree type of structure, so that significant sub-expressions can be readily isolated. In the LISP programming system, the bulk of available memory is used for storing S-expressions in the form of list structures. This type of memory organization frees the programmer from the necessity of allocating storage for the different sections of his program.

The second important part of the LISP language is the source language itself which specifies in what way the S-expressions are to be processed. This consists of recursive functions of S-expressions. Since the notation for the writing of recursive functions of S-expressions is itself outside the S-expression notation, it will be called the meta language. These expressions will therefore be called M-expressions.

Third, LISP can interpret and execute programs written in the form of S-expressions. Thus, like machine language, and unlike most other higher level languages, it can be used to generate programs for further execution.

1.1 Symbolic Expressions

The most elementary type of S-expression is the atomic symbol.

Definition: An atomic symbol is a string of no more than thirty numerals and capital letters; the first character must be a letter.

Examples

        A
        APPLE
        PART2
        EXTRALONGSTRINGOFLETTERS
        A4B66XYZ2

These symbols are called atomic because they are taken as a whole and are not capable of being split within LISP into individual characters. Thus A, B, and AB have no relation to each other except in so far as they are three distinct atomic symbols.

All S-expressions are built out of atomic symbols and the punctuation marks

"(", ") ", and " . ". The basic operation for forming S-expressions is to combine two of them to produce a larger one. From the two atomic symbols Al and A2, one can form the S-expression (A1 . A2).

Definition: An S-expression is either an atomic symbol or it is composed of these elements in the following order: a left parenthesis, an S-expression, a dot, an S-expression, and a right parenthesis.

Notice that this definition is recursive.

Examples

ATOM
(A . B)
(A . (B . C))
((A1 . A2) . B)
((U . V) . (X . Y))
((U . V) . (X . (Y . Z)))

1.2 Elementary Functions

We shall introduce some elementary functions of S-expressions. To distinguish the functions from the S-expressions themselves, we shall write function names in lower case letters, since atomic symbols consist of only upper case letters. Furthermore, the arguments of functions will be grouped in square brackets rather than parentheses. As a separator or punctuation mark we shall use the semicolon.

The first function that we shall introduce is the function cons. It has two arguments and is in fact the function that is used to build S-expressions from smaller S-expressions.

Examples

cons[A;B]=(A . B)
cons[(A . B);C]=((A . B) . C)
cons[cons[A;B];C]=((A . B) . C)

The last example is an instance of composition of functions. It is possible to build any S-expression from its atomic components by compositions of the function cons.

The next pair of functions do just the opposite of cons. They produce the subexpressions of a given expression.

The function car has one argument. Its value is the first part of its composite argument. car of an atomic symbol is undefined.

Examples

car[(A . B)]=A
car[(A . (B1 . B2))]=A
car[((A1 . A2) . B)]=(A1 . A2)
car[A] is undefined

The function cdr has one argument. Its value is the second part of its composite argument. cdr is also undefined if its argument is atomic.

Examples

cdr[(A . B)]=B

cdr[(A . (B1 . B2))]=(B1 . B2)

cdr[((A1 . A2) . B)]=B

cdr[A] is undefined

car[cdr[(A . (B1 . B2))]]=B1

car[cdr[(A . B)]] is undefined

car[cons[A;B]]=A

Given any S-expression, it is possible to produce any subexpression of it by a suitable composition of car's and cdr's. If x and y represent any two S-expressions, the following identities are true:

car[cons[x;y]]=x

cdr[cons[x;y]]=y

The following identity is also true for any S-expression x such that x is composite (non-atomic):

cons[car[x];cdr[x]]=x

The symbols x and y used in these identities are called variables. In LISP, variables are used to represent S-expressions. In choosing names for variables and functions, we shall use the same type of character strings that are used in forming atomic symbols, except that we shall use lower case letters.

A function whose value is either true or false is called a predicate. In LISP, the values true and false are represented by the atomic symbols T and F, respectively. A LISP predicate is therefore a function whose value is either T or F.

The predicate eq is a test for equality on atomic symbols. It is undefined for non-atomic arguments.

Examples

eq[A;A]=T

eq[A;B]=F

eq[A;(A . B)] is undefined

eq[(A . B);(A . B)] is undefined

The predicate atom is true if its argument is an atomic symbol, and false if its argument is composite.

Examples

atom[EXTRALONGSTRINGOFLETTERS]=T

atom[(U . V)]=F

atom[car[(U . V)]]=T

1.3 List Notation

The S-expressions that have been used heretofore have been written in dot notation. It is usually more convenient to be able to write lists of expressions of indefinite length, such as (A B C D E).

Any S-expression can be expressed in terms of the dot notation. However, LISP has an alternative form of S-expression called the list notation. The list $(m_1 m_2 \ldots m_n)$ can be defined in terms of dot notation. It is identical to $(m_1 . (m_2 . (\ldots . (m_n . NIL) \ldots)))$.

The atomic symbol NIL serves as a terminator for lists. The null list ( ) is identical to NIL. Lists may have sublists. The dot notation and the list notation may be used in the same S-expression.

Historically, the separator for elements of lists was the comma (,); however, the blank is now generally used. The two are entirely equivalent in LISP. (A, B, C) is identical to (A B C).

Examples

        (A B C)=(A . (B . (C . NIL)))
        ((A B) C)=((A . (B . NIL)) . (C . NIL))
        (A B (C D))=(A . (B . ((C . (D . NIL)) . NIL)))
        (A)=(A . NIL)
        ((A))=((A . NIL) . NIL)
        (A (B . C))=(A . ((B . C) . NIL))

It is important to become familiar with the results of elementary functions on S-expressions written in list notation. These can always be determined by translating into dot notation.

Examples

        car[(A B C)]=A
        cdr[(A B C)]=(B C)
        cons[A; (B C)]=(A B C)
        car[((A B) C)]=(A B)
        cdr[(A)]=NIL
        car[cdr[(A B C)]]=B

It is convenient to abbreviate multiple car's and cdr's. This is done by forming function names that begin with c, end with r, and have several a's and d's between them.

Examples

        cadr[(A B C)]=car[cdr[(A B C)]]=B
        caddr[(A B C)]=C
        cadadr[(A (B C) D)]=C

4

The last a or d in the name actually signifies the first operation in order to be performed, since it is nearest to the argument.

1.4 The LISP Meta-language

We have introduced a type of data called S-expressions, and five elementary functions of S-expressions. We have also discussed the following features of the meta-language.

1. Function names and variable names are like atomic symbols except that they use lower case letters.

2. The arguments of a function are bound by square brackets and separated from each other by semicolons.

3. Compositions of functions may be written by using nested sets of brackets.

These rules allow one to write function definitions such as

$$third[x] = car[cdr[cdr[x]]].$$

This function selects the third item on a list. For example,

$$third[(A \ B \ C \ D)] = C$$

third is actually the same function as caddr.

The class of functions that can be formed in this way is quite limited and not very interesting. A much larger class of functions can be defined by means of the conditional expression, a device for providing branches in function definitions.

A conditional expression has the following form:

$$[p_1 \rightarrow e_1; \ p_2 \rightarrow e_2; \ \dots; \ p_n \rightarrow e_n],$$

where each p_i is an expression whose value may be truth or falsity, and each e_i is any expression. The meaning of a conditional expression is: if p_1 is true, then the value of e_1 is the value of the entire expression. If p_1 is false, then if p_2 is true the value of e_2 is the value of the entire expression. The p_i are searched from left to right until the first true one is found. Then the corresponding e_i is selected. If none of the p_i are true, then the value of the entire expression is undefined.

Each p_i or e_i can itself be either an S-expression, a function, a composition of functions or may itself be another conditional expression.

Example

$$[eq[car[x];A] \rightarrow cons[B;cdr[x]]; \ T \rightarrow x]$$

The atomic symbol T represents truth. The value of this expression is obtained if one replaces car of x by B if it happens to be A, but leaving x unchanged if car of it is not A.

The main application of conditional expressions is in defining functions recursively.

Example

$$ff[x]=[atom[x]\rightarrow x;\ T\rightarrow ff[car[x]]]$$

This example defines the function ff which selects the first atomic symbol of any given expression. This expression can be read: If x is an atomic symbol, then x itself is the answer. Otherwise the function ff is to be applied to car of x.

If x is atomic, then the first branch which is " x " will be selected. Otherwise, the second branch "ff[car[x]]" will be selected, since T is always true.

The definition of ff is recursive in that ff is actually defined in terms of itself. If one keeps taking car of any S-expression, one will eventually produce an atomic symbol; therefore the process is always well defined.

Some recursive functions may be well defined for certain arguments only, but infinitely recursive for certain other arguments. When such a function is interpreted in the LISP programming system, it will either use up all of the available memory, or loop until the program is halted artificially.

We shall now work out the evaluation of ff[((A . B) . C)]. First, we substitute the arguments in place of the variable x in the definition and obtain

$$ff[((A\ .\ B)\ .\ C)]=[atom[((A\ .\ B)\ .\ C)]\rightarrow((A\ .\ B)\ .\ C);\ T\rightarrow ff[car[((A\ .\ B)\ .\ C)]]]$$

but ((A . B) . C) is not atomic, and so we have

$$= [T\rightarrow ff[car[((A\ .\ B)\ .\ C)]]]$$
$$= ff[car[((A\ .\ B)\ .\ C)]]$$
$$= ff[(A\ .\ B)]$$

At this point, the definition of ff must be used recursively. Substituting (A . B) for x gives

$$= [atom[(A\ .\ B)]\rightarrow(A\ .\ B);\ T\rightarrow ff[car[(A\ .\ B)]]]$$
$$= [T\rightarrow ff[car[(A\ .\ B)]]]$$
$$= ff[car[(A\ .\ B)]]$$
$$= ff[A]$$
$$= [atom[A]\rightarrow A;\ T\rightarrow ff[car[A]]]$$
$$= A$$

The conditional expression is useful for defining numerical computations, as well as computations with S-expressions. The absolute value of a number can be defined by

$$|x|=[x<0\rightarrow-x;\ T\rightarrow x].$$

The factorial of a non-negative integer can be defined by

$$n!=[n=0\rightarrow1;\ T\rightarrow n\cdot[n-1]!]$$

This recursive definition does not terminate for negative arguments. A function that is defined only for certain arguments is called a partial function.

The Euclidean algorithm for finding the greatest common divisor of two positive integers can be defined by using conditional expressions as follows:

$$\gcd[x;y]=[x{>}y{\rightarrow}\gcd[y;x];$$
$$\text{rem}[y;x]{=}0{\rightarrow}x;$$
$$T{\rightarrow}\gcd[\text{rem}[y;x];x]]$$

$\underline{\text{rem}[u;v]}$ is the remainder when $\underline{u}$ is divided by $\underline{v}$.

A detailed discussion of the theory of functions defined recursively by conditional expressions is found in " A Basis for a Mathematical Theory of Computation " by J. McCarthy, Proceedings of the Western Joint Computer Conference, May 1961 (published by the Institute of Radio Engineers).

It is usual for most mathematicians—exclusive of those devoted to logic—to use the word " function " imprecisely, and to apply it to forms such as $\underline{y^2{+}x}$. Because we shall later compute with expressions that stand for functions, we need a notation that expresses the distinction between functions and forms. The notation that we shall use is the lambda notation of Alonzo Church.[1]

Let $\underline{f}$ be an expression that stands for a function of two integer variables. It should make sense to write $\underline{f[3;4]}$ and to be able to determine the value of this expression. For example, $\underline{\text{sum}[3;4]{=}7}$. The expression $\underline{y^2{+}x}$ does not meet this requirement. It is not at all clear whether the value of $\underline{y^2{+}x[3;4]}$ is 13 or 19. An expression such as $\underline{y^2{+}x}$ will be called a form rather than a function. A form can be converted to a function by specifying the correspondence between the variables in the form and the arguments of the desired function.

If ϵ is a form in the variables $x_1;\ldots;x_n$, then the expression $\lambda[[x_1;\ldots;x_n];\epsilon]$ represents the function of n variables obtained by substituting the n arguments in order for the variables $x_1;\ldots;x_n$, respectively. For example, the function $\lambda[[x;y];y^2{+}x]$ is a function of two variables, and $\lambda[[x;y];y^2{+}x][3;4]{=}4^2{+}3{=}19$. $\lambda[[y;x];y^2{+}x][3;4]{=}3^2{+}4{=}13$.

The variables in a lambda expression are dummy or bound variables because systematically changing them does not alter the meaning of the expression. Thus $\lambda[[u;v];v^2{+}u]$ means the same thing as $\lambda[[x;y];y^2{+}x]$.

We shall sometimes use expressions in which a variable is not bound by a lambda. For example, in the function of two variables $\lambda[[x;y];x^n{+}y^n]$ the variable n is not bound. This is called a free variable. It may be regarded as a parameter. Unless n has been given a value before trying to compute with this function, the value of the function must be undefined.

---

1. A. Church, The Calculi of Lambda-Conversion (Princeton University Press, Princeton, New Jersey, 1941).

The lambda notation alone is inadequate for naming recursive functions. Not only must the variables be bound, but the name of the function must be bound, since it is used inside an expression to stand for the entire expression. The function ff was previously defined by the identity

ff[x]=[atom[x]→x; T→ff[car[x]]].

Using the lambda notation, we can write

ff=λ[[x];[atom[x]→x; T→ff[car[x]]]]

The equality sign in these identities is actually not part of the LISP meta-language and is only a crutch until we develop the correct notation. The right side of the last equation cannot serve as an expression for the function ff because there is nothing to indicate that the occurrence of ff inside it stands for the function that is being defined.

In order to be able to write expressions that bear their own name, we introduce the label notation. If ε is an expression, and α is its name, we write label[α;ε].

The function ff can now be written without an equal sign:

label[ff;λ[[x];[atom[x]→x; T→ff[car[x]]]]]

In this expression, x is a bound variable, and ff is a bound function name.

1.5 Syntactic Summary[1]

All parts of the LISP language have now been explained. That which follows is a complete syntactic definition of the LISP language, together with semantic comments. The definition is given in Backus notation[2] with the addition of three dots(...) to avoid naming unneccessary syntactic types.

In Backus notation the symbols "::=", "<", ">", and "|" are used. The rule <S-expression>::=<atomic symbol>|(<S-expression> . <S-expression>) means that an S-expression is either an atomic symbol, or it is a left parenthesis followed by an S-expression followed by a dot followed by an S-expression followed by a right parenthesis. The vertical bar means "or", and the angular brackets always enclose elements of the syntax that is being defined.

The Data Language

```
<LETTER>::=A|B|C|...|Z
<number>::=0|1|2|...|9
<atomic-symbol>::=<LETTER><atom part>
<atom part>::=<empty>|<LETTER><atom part>|<number><atom part>
```

Atomic symbols are the smallest entities in LISP. Their decomposition into characters has no significance.

---

1. This section is for completeness and may be skipped upon first reading.
2. J. W. Backus, The Syntax and Semantics of the Proposed International Algebraic Language of the Zurich ACM-Gamm Conference. ICIP Paris, June 1959.

```
<S-expression>::=<atomic symbol>|
                 (<S-expression>.<S-expression>)|
                 (<S-expression>...<S-expression>)
```

When three dots are used in this manner, they mean that any number of the given type of symbol may occur, including none at all. According to this rule, ( ) is a valid S-expression. (It is equivalent to NIL.)

The dot notation is the fundamental notation of S-expressions, although the list notation is often more convenient. Any S-expression can be written in dot notation.

The Meta-Language

```
<letter>::=a|b|c|...|z
<identifier>::=<letter><id part>
<id part>::=<empty>| <letter><id part>| <number><id part>
```

The names of functions and variables are formed in the same manner as atomic symbols but with lower-case letters.

```
<form>::=<constant>|
         <variable>|
         <function>[<argument>; ...;<argument>]|
         [<form>→<form>; ...;<form>→<form>]
<constant>::=<S-expression>
<variable>::=<identifier>
<argument>::=<form>
```

A form is an expression that can be evaluated. A form that is merely a constant has that constant as its value. If a form is a variable, then the value of the form is the S-expression that is bound to that variable at the time when we evaluate the form.

The third part of this rule states that we may write a function followed by a list of arguments separated by semicolons and enclosed in square brackets. The expressions for the arguments are themselves forms; this indicates that compositions of functions are permitted.

The last part of this rule gives the format of the conditional expression. This is evaluated by evaluating the forms in the propositional position in order until one is found whose value is T. Then the form after the arrow is evaluated and gives the value of the entire expression.

```
<function>::=<identifier>|
             λ[<var list>;<form>]|
             label[<identifier>;<function>]
<var list>::=[<variable>; ...;<variable>]
```

A function can be simply a name. In this case its meaning must be previously understood. A function may be defined by using the lambda notation and establishing a correspondence between the arguments and the variables used in a form. If the function is recursive, it must be given a name by using a label.

1.6 A Universal LISP Function

An interpreter or universal function is one that can compute the value of any given function applied to its arguments when given a description of that function. (Of course, if the function that is being interpreted has infinite recursion, the interpreter will recur infinitely also.)

We are now in a position to define the universal LISP function evalquote[fn;args]. When evalquote is given a function and a list of arguments for that function, it computes the value of the function applied to the arguments.

LISP functions have S-expressions as arguments. In particular, the argument "fn" of the function evalquote must be an S-expression. Since we have been writing functions as M-expressions, it is necessary to translate them into S-expressions.

The following rules define a method of translating functions written in the meta-language into S-expressions.

1. If the function is represented by its name, it is translated by changing all of the letters to upper case, making it an atomic symbol. Thus car is translated to CAR.

2. If the function uses the lambda notation, then the expression $\lambda[[x_1;...;x_n];\epsilon]$ is translated into (LAMBDA (X1 ... XN) ϵ*), where ϵ* is the translation of ϵ.

3. If the function begins with label, then the translation of label[a;ϵ] is (LABEL a* ϵ*).

Forms are translated as follows:

1. A variable, like a function name, is translated by using uppercase letters. Thus the translation of var1 is VAR1.

2. The obvious translation of letting a constant translate into itself will not work. Since the translation of x is X, the translation of X must be something else to avoid ambiguity. The solution is to quote it. Thus X is translated into (QUOTE X).

3. The form fn[arg_1;...;arg_n] is translated into (fn* arg_1* ... arg_n*)

4. The conditional expression [$p_1 \rightarrow e_1$;...;$p_n \rightarrow e_n$] is translated into (COND (p_1* e_1*) ... (p_n* e_n*)).

Examples

M-expressions	S-expressions
x	X
car	CAR
car[x]	(CAR X)
T	(QUOTE T)
ff [car [x]]	(FF (CAR X))
[atom[x]→x; T→ff[car[x]]]	(COND ((ATOM X) X) ((QUOTE T) (FF (CAR X))))
label[ff;λ[[x];[atom[x]→x; T→ff[car[x]]]]]	(LABEL FF (LAMBDA (X) (COND ((ATOM X) X) ((QUOTE T) (FF (CAR X))))))

Some useful functions for handling S-expressions are given below. Some of them are needed as auxiliary functions for <u>evalquote</u>.

<u>equal</u>[x;y]

This is a predicate that is true if its two arguments are identical S-expressions, and is false if they are different. (The elementary predicate <u>eq</u> is defined only for atomic arguments.) The definition of <u>equal</u> is an example of a conditional expression inside a conditional expression.

$$equal[x;y] = [atom[x] \rightarrow [atom[y] \rightarrow eq[x;y];\ T \rightarrow F];$$
$$equal[car[x];car[y]] \rightarrow equal[cdr[x];cdr[y]];$$
$$T \rightarrow F]$$

This can be translated into the following S-expression:

```
(LABEL EQUAL (LAMBDA (X Y) (COND
    ((ATOM X) (COND ((ATOM Y) (EQ X Y)) ((QUOTE T) (QUOTE F))))
    ((EQUAL (CAR X) (CAR Y)) (EQUAL (CDR X) (CDR Y)))
    ((QUOTE T) (QUOTE F))      )))
```

<u>subst</u>[x;y;z]

This function gives the result of substituting the S-expression x for all occurrences of the atomic symbol y in the S-expression z. It is defined by

$$subst[x;y;z] = [equal[y;z] \rightarrow x; atom[z] \rightarrow z; T \rightarrow cons[subst$$
$$[x;y;car[z]]; subst[x;y;cdr[z]]]]$$

As an example, we have

$$subst[(X . A); B; ((A . B) . C)] = ((A . (X . A)) . C)$$

<u>null</u>[x]

This predicate is useful for deciding when a list is exhausted. It is true if and only if its argument is NIL.

The following functions are useful when S-expressions are regarded as lists.

1. <u>append</u>[x;y]

$$append[x;y] = [null[x] \rightarrow y; T \rightarrow cons[car[x]; append[cdr[x];y]]]$$

An example is

$$append[(A\ B);(C\ D\ E)] = (A\ B\ C\ D\ E)$$

2. <u>member</u>[x;y]

This predicate is true if the S-expression x occurs among the elements of the list y. We have

$$member[x;y] = [null[y] \rightarrow F;$$
$$equal[x;car[y]] \rightarrow T;$$
$$T \rightarrow member[x;cdr[y]]]$$

3. <u>pairlis</u>[x;y;a]

This function gives the list of pairs of corresponding elements of the lists x and y, and appends this to the list a. The resultant list of pairs, which is like a table with two columns, is called an association list. We have

pairlis[x;y;a] = [null[x]→a;T→cons[cons[car[x];car[y]];
          pairlis[cdr[x];cdr[y];a]]]

An example is

pairlis[(A B C);(U V W);((D . X) (E . Y))] =
          ((A . U) (B . V) (C . W) (D . X) (E . Y))

4. <u>assoc[x;a]</u>

If a is an association list such as the one formed by pairlis in the above example, then assoc will produce the first pair whose first term is x. Thus it is a table searching function. We have

assoc[x;a] = [equal[caar[a];x]→car[a];T→assoc[x;cdr[a]]]

An example is

assoc[B;((A . (M N)), (B . (CAR X)), (C . (QUOTE M)), (C . (CDR X)))]
= (B . (CAR X))

5. <u>sublis[a;y]</u>

Here a is assumed to be an association list of the form $((u_1 . v_1) ... (u_n . v_n))$, where the u's are atomic, and y is any S-expression. What sublis does, is to treat the u's as variables when they occur in y, and to substitute the corresponding v's from the pair list. In order to define sublis, we first define an auxiliary function. We have

sub2[a;z] = [null[a]→z;eq[caar[a];z]→cdar[a];T→
          sub2[cdr[a];z]]

and

sublis[a;y] = [atom[y]→sub2[a;y];T→cons[sublis[a;car[y]];
          sublis[a;cdr[y]]]]

An example is

sublis[((X . SHAKESPEARE) (Y . (THE TEMPEST)));(X WROTE Y)] =
          (SHAKESPEARE WROTE (THE TEMPEST))

The universal function <u>evalquote</u> that is about to be defined obeys the following identity. Let <u>f</u> be a function written as an M-expression, and let <u>fn</u> be its translation. (<u>fn</u> is an S-expression.) Let <u>f</u> be a function of n arguments and let args=$(arg_1 ... arg_n)$, a list of the n S-expressions being used as arguments. Then

evalquote[fn;args]=f[arg_1;...;arg_n]

if either side of the equation is defined at all.

Example

$$
\begin{aligned}
&\text{f:} && \lambda[[x;y];\text{cons}[\text{car}[x];y]] \\
&\text{fn:} && (\text{LAMBDA } (X\ Y) (\text{CONS } (\text{CAR } X)\ Y)) \\
&\text{arg}_1\text{:} && (A\ B) \\
&\text{arg}_2\text{:} && (C\ D) \\
&\text{args:} && ((A\ B)\ (C\ D))
\end{aligned}
$$

evalquote[(LAMBDA (X Y) (CONS (CAR X) Y)); ((A B) (C D))] =
$\lambda[[x;y];\text{cons}[\text{car}[x];y]][(A\ B);(C\ D)]$=
(A C D)

evalquote is defined by using two main functions, called <u>eval</u> and <u>apply</u>. <u>apply</u> handles a function and its arguments, while <u>eval</u> handles forms. Each of these functions also has another argument that is used as an association list for storing the values of bound variables and function names.

evalquote[fn;x] = apply[fn;x;NIL]

where

apply[fn;x;a] =
　[atom[fn] → [eq[fn;CAR] → caar[x];
　　　　　　eq[fn;CDR] → cdar[x];
　　　　　　eq[fn;CONS] → cons[car[x];cadr[x]];
　　　　　　eq[fn;ATOM] → atom[car[x]];
　　　　　　eq[fn;EQ] → eq[car[x];cadr[x]];
　　　　　　T → apply[eval[fn;a];x;a]];
　　eq[car[fn];LAMBDA] → eval[caddr[fn];pairlis[cadr[fn];x;a]];
　　eq[car[fn];LABEL] → apply[caddr[fn];x;cons[cons[cadr[fn];
　　　　　　　　　　　　　　　　　　　　caddr[fn]];a]]]

eval[e;a] = [atom[e] → cdr[assoc[e;a]];
　　atom[car[e]] →
　　　　　[eq[car[e];QUOTE] → cadr[e];
　　　　　eq[car[e];COND] → evcon[cdr[e];a];
　　　　　T → apply[car[e];evlis[cdr[e];a];a]];
　　T → apply[car[e];evlis[cdr[e];a];a]]

pairlis and assoc have been previously defined.

evcon[c;a] = [eval[caar[c];a] → eval[cadar[c];a];
　　　　T → evcon[cdr[c];a]]

and
　evlis[m;a] = [null[m] → NIL;
　　　　T → cons[eval[car[m];a];evlis[cdr[m];a]]]

13

We shall explain a number of points about these definitions.

The first argument for <u>apply</u> is a function. If it is an atomic symbol, then there are two possibilities. One is that it is an elementary function: <u>car</u>, <u>cdr</u>, <u>cons</u>, <u>eq</u>. or <u>atom</u>. In each case, the appropriate function is applied to the argument(s). If it is not one of these, then its meaning has to be looked up in the association list.

If it begins with LAMBDA, then the arguments are paired with the bound variables, and the form is given to <u>eval</u> to evaluate.

If it begins with LABEL, then the function name and definition are added to the association list, and the inside function is evaluated by <u>apply</u>.

The first argument of <u>eval</u> is a form. If it is atomic, then it must be a variable, and its value is looked up on the association list.

If <u>car</u> of the form is QUOTE, then it is a constant, and the value is <u>cadr</u> of the form itself.

If <u>car</u> of the form is COND, then it is a conditional expression, and <u>evcon</u> evaluates the propositional terms in order, and choses the form following the first true predicate.

In all other cases, the form must be a function followed by its arguments. The arguments are then evaluated, and the function is given to <u>apply</u>.

The LISP Programming System has many added features that have not been described thus far. These will be treated hereafter. At this point, it is worth noting the following points.

1. In the pure theory of LISP, all functions other than the five basic ones need to be defined each time they are to be used. This is unworkable in a practical sense. The LISP programming system has a larger stock of built-in functions known to the interpreter, and provision for adding as many more as the programmer cares to define.

2. The basic functions <u>car</u>, and <u>cdr</u> were said to be undefined for atomic arguments. In the system, they always have a value, although it may not always be meaningful. Similarly, the basic predicate <u>eq</u> always has a value. The effects of these functions in unusual cases will be understood after reading the chapter on list structures in the computer.

3. Except for very unusual cases, one never writes (QUOTE T) or (QUOTE F), but T, and F respectively.

4. There is provision in LISP for computing with fixed and floating point numbers. These are introduced as psuedo-atomic symbols.

The reader is warned that the definitions of <u>apply</u> and <u>eval</u> given above are pedagogical devices and are not the same functions as those built into the LISP programming system. Appendix B contains the computer implemented version of these functions and should be used to decide questions about how things really work.

II. THE LISP INTERPRETER SYSTEM

The following example is a LISP program that defines three functions union, inter-section, and member, and then applies these functions to some test cases. The functions union and intersection are to be applied to "sets," each set being represented by a list of atomic symbols. The functions are defined as follows. Note that they are all recursive, and both union and intersection make use of member.

member[a;x] = [null[x]→F;eq[a;car[x]]→T;T→
member[a;cdr[x]]]

union[x;y] = [null[x]→y;member[car[x];y]→union
[cdr[x];y];T→cons[car[x];union[cdr[x];y]]]

intersection[x;y] = [null[x]→NIL;member[car[x];y]
→cons[car[x];intersection[cdr[x];y]];T→
intersection[cdr[x];y]]

To define these functions, we use the pseudo-function define. The program looks like this:

```
DEFINE ((
(MEMBER (LAMBDA (A X) (COND ((NULL X) F)
     ( (EQ A (CAR X) ) T) (T (MEMBER A (CDR X))) )))
(UNION (LAMBDA (X Y) (COND ((NULL X) Y) ((MEMBER
     (CAR X) Y) (UNION (CDR X) Y)) (T (CONS (CAR X)
     (UNION (CDR X) Y))) )))
(INTERSECTION (LAMBDA (X Y) (COND ((NULL X) NIL)
     ( (MEMBER (CAR X) Y) (CONS (CAR X) (INTERSECTION
     (CDR X) Y))) (T (INTERSECTION (CDR X) Y)) )))
))
INTERSECTION ((A1 A2 A3) (A1 A3 A5))
UNION ((X Y Z) (U V W X))
```

This program contains three distinct functions for the LISP interpreter. The first function is the pseudo-function define. A pseudo-function is a function that is executed for its effect on the system in core memory, as well as for its value. define causes these functions to be defined and available within the system. Its value is a list of the functions defined, in this case (MEMBER UNION INTERSECTION).

The value of the second function is (A1 A3). The value of the third function is (Y Z U V W X). An inspection of the way in which the recursion is carried out will show why the "elements" of the "set" appear in just this order.

Following are some elementary rules for writing LISP 1.5 programs.

1. A program for execution in LISP consists of a sequence of doublets. The first list or atomic symbol of each doublet is interpreted as a function. The second is a list

of arguments for the function. They are evaluated by <u>evalquote</u>, and the value is printed.

2. There is no particular card format for writing LISP. Columns 1-72 of any number of cards may be used. Card boundaries are ignored. The format of this program, including indentation, was chosen merely for ease of reading.

3. A comma is the equivalent of a blank. Any number of blanks and/or commas can occur at any point in a program except in the middle of an atomic symbol.

4. Do not use the forms (QUOTE T), (QUOTE F), and (QUOTE NIL). Use T, F, and NIL instead.

5. Atomic symbols should begin with alphabetical characters to distinguish them from numbers.

6. Dot notation may be used in LISP 1.5. Any number of blanks before or after the dot will be ignored.

7. Dotted pairs may occur as elements of a list, and lists may occur as elements of dotted pairs. For example,

((A . B) X (C . (E F G)))

is a valid S-expression. It could also be written

((A . B) . (X . ((C . (E . (F . (G . NIL)))) . NIL))) or
((A . B) X (C E F G))

8. A form of the type (A B C . D) is an abbreviation for (A . (B . (C . D))). Any other mixing of commas (spaces) and dots on the same level is an error, e.g. (A . B C).

9. A selection of basic functions is provided with the LISP system. Other functions may be introduced by the programmer. The order in which functions are introduced is not significant. Any function may make use of any other function.

2.1 Variables

A variable is a symbol that is used to represent an argument of a function. Thus one might write "a + b, where a = 341 and b = 216." In this situation no confusion can result and all will agree that the answer is 557. In order to arrive at this result, it is necessary to substitute the actual numbers for the variables, and then add the two number (on an adding machine for instance).

One reason why there is no ambiguity in this case is that "a" and "b" are not acceptable inputs for an adding machine, and it is therefore obvious that they merely represent the actual arguments. In LISP, the situation can be much more complicated. An atomic symbol may be either a variable or an actual argument. To further complicate the situation, a part of an argument may be a variable when a function inside another function is evaluated. The intuitive approach is no longer adequate. An understanding of the formalism in use is necessary to do any effective LISP programming.

Lest the prospective LISP user be discouraged at this point, it should be pointed out that nothing new is going to be introduced here. This section is intended to reinforce the discussion of Section I. Everything in this section can be derived from the rule for

16

translating M-expressions into S-expressions, or alternatively everything in this section can be inferred from the universal function evalquote of Section I.

The formalism for variables in LISP is the Church lambda notation. The part of the interpreter that binds variables is called apply. When apply encounters a function beginning with LAMBDA, the list of variables is paired with the list of arguments and added to the front of the a-list. During the evaluation of the function, variables may be encountered. They are evaluated by looking them up on the a-list. If a variable has been bound several times, the last or most recent value is used. The part of the interpreter that does this is called eval. The following example will illustrate this discussion. Suppose the interpreter is given the following doublet:

   fn: (LAMBDA (X Y) (CONS X Y))

   args: (A B)

evalquote will give these arguments to apply. (Look at the universal function of Section I.)

   apply[(LAMBDA (X Y) (CONS X Y)); (A B);NIL]

apply will bind the variables and give the function and a-list to eval.

   eval[(CONS X Y); ((X . A) (Y . B))]

eval will evaluate the variables and give it to cons.

   cons[A;B] = (A . B)

The actual interpreter skips one step required by the universal function, namely, apply[CONS;(A B);((X . A) (Y . B))].

2.2 Constants

It is sometimes assumed that a constant stands for itself as opposed to a variable which stands for something else. This is not a very workable concept, since the student who is learning calculus is taught to represent constants by a, b, c... and variables by x, y, z.... . It seems more reasonable to say that one variable is more nearly constant than another if it is bound at a higher level and changes value less frequently.

In LISP, a variable remains bound within the scope of the LAMBDA that binds it. When a variable always has a certain value regardless of the current a-list, it will be called a constant. This is accomplished by means of the property list[1] (p-list) of the variable symbol. Every atomic symbol has a p-list. When the p-list contains the indicator APVAL, then the symbol is a constant and the next item on the list is the value. eval searches p-lists before a-lists when evaluating variables, thus making it possible to set constants.

Constants can be made by the programmer. To make the variable X always stand for (A B C D), use the pseudo-function cset.

---

1. Property lists are discussed in Section VII.

cset[X;(A B C D)]

An interesting type of constant is one that stands for itself. NIL is an example of this. It can be evaluated repeatedly and will still be NIL. T, F, NIL, and other constants cannot be used as variables.

2.3 Functions

When a symbol stands for a function, the situation is similar to that in which a symbol stands for an argument. When a function is recursive, it must be given a name. This is done by means of the form LABEL, which pairs the name with the function definition on the a-list. The name is then bound to the function definition, just as a variable is bound to its value.

In actual practice, LABEL is seldom used. It is usually more convenient to attach the name to the definition in a uniform manner. This is done by putting on the property list of the name, the symbol EXPR followed by the function definition. The pseudo-function define used at the beginning of this section accomplishes this. When apply interprets a function represented by an atomic symbol, it searches the p-list of the atomic symbol before searching the current a-list. Thus a define will override a LABEL.

The fact that most functions are constants defined by the programmer, and not variables that are modified by the program, is not due to any weakness of the system. On the contrary, it indicates a richness of the system which we do not know how to exploit very well.

2.4 Machine Language Functions

Some functions instead of being defined by S-expressions are coded as closed machine language subroutines. Such a function will have the indicator SUBR on its property list followed by a pointer that allows the interpreter to link with the subroutine. There are three ways in which a subroutine can be present in the system.

1. The subroutine is coded into the LISP system.

2. The function is hand-coded by the user in the assembly type language, LAP.

3. The function is first defined by an S-expression, and then compiled by the LISP compiler. Compiled functions run from 10 to 100 times as fast as they do when they are interpreted.

2.5 Special Forms

Normally, eval evaluates the arguments of a function before applying the function itself. Thus if eval is given (CONS X Y), it will evaluate X and Y, and then cons them. But if eval is given (QUOTE X), X should not be evaluated. QUOTE is a special form that prevents its argument from being evaluated.

A special form differs from a function in two ways. Its arguments are not evaluated before the special form sees them. COND, for example, has a very special way of

18

evaluating its arguments by using _evcon_. The second way which special forms differ from functions is that they may have an indefinite number of arguments. Special forms have indicators on their property lists called FEXPR and FSUBR for LISP-defined forms and machine language coded forms, respectively.

2.6 Programming for the Interpreter

The purpose of this section is to help the programmer avoid certain common errors.

Example 1

    fn: CAR
    args: ((A B))

The value is A. Note that the interpreter expects a list of arguments. The one argument for _car_ is (A B). The extra pair of parentheses is necessary.

One could write (LAMBDA (X) (CAR X)) instead of just CAR. This is correct but unnecessary.

Example 2

    fn: CONS
    args: (A (B . C))

The value is cons$[A;(B . C)]$ = (A . (B . C)).
The print program will write this as (A B . C).

Example 3

    fn: CONS
    args: ((CAR (QUOTE (A . B))) (CDR (QUOTE (C . D))))

The value of this computation will be ((CAR (QUOTE (A . B))) . (CDR (QUOTE (C . D)))). This is not what the programmer expected. He expected (CAR (QUOTE (A . B))) to evaluate to A, and expected (A . D) as the value of cons.

The interpreter expects a list of arguments. It does not expect a list of expressions that will evaluate to the arguments. Two correct ways of writing this function are listed below. The first one makes the _car_ and _cdr_ part of a function specified by a LAMBDA. The second one uses quoted arguments and gets them evaluated by _eval_ with a null a-list.

    fn: (LAMBDA (X Y) (CONS (CAR X) (CDR Y)))
    args: ((A . B) (C . D))
    fn: EVAL
    args: ((CONS (CAR (QUOTE (A . B))) (CDR (QUOTE (C . D)))) NIL)

The value of both of these is (A . D).

III. EXTENSION OF THE LISP LANGUAGE

Section I of this manual presented a purely formal mathematical system that we shall call pure LISP. The elements of this formal system are the following.

1. A set of symbols called S-expressions.

2. A functional notation called M-expressions.

3. A formal mapping of M-expressions into S-expressions.

4. A universal function (written as an M-expression) for interpreting the application of any function written as an S-expression to its arguments.

Section II introduced the LISP Programming System. The basis of the LISP Programming System is the interpreter, or <u>evalquote</u> and its components. A LISP program in fact consists of pairs of arguments for <u>evalquote</u> which are interpreted in sequence.

In this section we shall introduce a number of extensions of elementary LISP. These extensions of elementary LISP are of two sorts. The first includes propositional connectives and functions with functions as arguments, and they are also of a mathematical nature; the second is peculiar to the LISP Programming System on the IBM 7090 computer.

In all cases, additions to the LISP Programming System are made to conform to the functional syntax of LISP even though they are not functions. For example, the command to print an S-expression on the output tape is called <u>print</u>. Syntactically, <u>print</u> is a function of one argument. It may be used in composition with other functions, and will be evaluated in the usual manner, with the inside of the composition being evaluated first. Its effect is to print its argument on the output tape (or on-line). It is a function only in the trivial sense that its value happens to be its argument, thus making it an identity function.

Commands to effect an action such as the operation of input-output, or the defining functions <u>define</u> and <u>cset</u> discussed in Chapter II, will be called pseudo-functions. It is characteristic of the LISP system that all functions including psuedo-functions must have values. In some cases the value is trivial and may be ignored.

This Chapter is concerned with several extensions of the LISP language that are in the system.

3.1 Functional Arguments

Mathematically, it is possible to have functions as arguments of other functions. For example, in arithmetic one could define a function <u>operate</u> [op;a;b], where op is a functional argument that specifies which arithmetic operation is to be performed on a and b. Thus

operate[+;3;4]=7   and
operate[x;3;4]=12

In LISP, functional arguments are extremely useful. A very important function with a functional argument is <u>maplist</u>. Its M-expression definition is maplist[x;fn]=[null[x]→NIL;

         T→cons[fn[x];maplist[cdr[x];fn]]]

An examination of the universal function <u>evalquote</u> will show that the interpreter can handle <u>maplist</u> and other functions written in this manner without any further addition. The functional argument is, of course, a function translated into an S-expression. It is bound to the variable <u>fn</u> and is then used whenever <u>fn</u> is mentioned as a function. The S-expression for <u>maplist</u> itself is as follows:

(MAPLIST (LAMBDA (X FN) (COND ((NULL X) NIL)
    (T (CONS (FN X) (MAPLIST (CDR X) FN))))))

Now suppose we wish to define a function that takes a list and changes it by <u>cons</u>-ing an X onto every item of the list so that, for example,

change[(A B (C D))]=((A . X) (B . X) ((C . D) . X))

Using <u>maplist</u>, we define <u>change</u> by

change[a]=maplist[a;λ[[j];cons[car[j];X]]]

This is not a valid M-expression as defined syntactically in section 1.5 because a function appears where a form is expected. This can be corrected by modifying the rule defining an argument so as to include functional arguments:

    <argument>:: = <form>|<function>

We also need a special rule to translate functional arguments into S-expression. If <u>fn</u> is a function used as an argument, then it is translated into (FUNCTION fn*).

Example

    (CHANGE (LAMBDA (A) (MAPLIST A (FUNCTION
        (LAMBDA (J) (CONS (CAR J) (QUOTE X))))))

An examination of evalquote shows that QUOTE will work instead of FUNCTION, <u>provided</u> that there are no free variables present. An explanation of how the interpreter processes the atomic symbol FUNCTION is given in the Appendix B.

3.2 Logical Connectives

The logical or Boolian connectives are usually considered as primitive operators. However, in LISP, they can be defined by using conditional expressions:

p∧q=[p→q;T→F]

p∨q=[p→T;T→q]

  ~q=[q→F;T→T]

In the System, <u>not</u> is a predicate of one argument. However, <u>and</u> and <u>or</u> are predicates of an indefinite number of arguments, and therefore are special forms. In writing M-expressions it is often convenient to use infix notation and write expressions such as a∨b∨c for or[a;b;c]. In S-expressions, one must, of course, use prefix notation and write (OR A B C).

The order in which the arguments of and and or are given may be of some significance in the case in which some of the arguments may not be well defined. The definitions of these predicated given above show that the value may be defined even if all of the arguments are not.

and evaluates its arguments from left to right. If one of them is found that is false, then the value of the and is false and no further arguments are evaluated. If the arguments are all evaluated and found to be true, then the value is true.

or evaluates its arguments from left to right. If one of them is true, then the value of the or is true and no further arguments are evaluated. If the arguments are all evaluated and found to be false, then the value is false.

3.3 Predicates and Truth in LISP

Although the rule for translating M-expressions into S-expressions states that T is (QUOTE T), it was stated that in the system one must always write T instead. Similarly, one must write F rather than (QUOTE F). The programmer may either accept this rule blindly or understand the following Humpty-Dumpty semantics.

In the LISP programming system there are two atomic symbols that represent truth and falsity respectively. These two atomic symbols are *T* and NIL. It is these symbols rather than T and F that are the actual value of all predicates in the system. This is mainly a coding convenience.

The atomic symbols T and F have APVAL's whose values are *T* and NIL, respectively. The symbols T and F for constant predicates will work because:

eval[T;NIL]=*T*
eval[F;NIL]=NIL

The forms (QUOTE *T*) and (QUOTE NIL) will also work because

eval[(QUOTE *T*);NIL]=*T*
eval[(QUOTE NIL);NIL]=NIL

T and NIL both have APVAL's that point to themselves. Thus *T* and NIL are also acceptable because

eval[*T*;NIL]=*T*
eval[NIL;NIL]=NIL

But

eval[(QUOTE F);NIL]=F

which is wrong and this is why (QUOTE F) will not work. Note that eval[(QUOTE T);alist]=T

which is wrong but will work for a different reason that will be explained in the paragraph after next.

There is no formal distinction between a function and a predicate in LISP. A predicate can be defined as a function whose value is either *T* or NIL. This is true of all predicates in the System.

One may use a form that is not a predicate in a location in which a predicate is called for, such as in the p position of a conditional expression, or as an argument of a logical predicate. Semantically, any S-expression that is not NIL will be regarded as truth in such a case. One consequence of this is that the predicates null and not are identical. Another consequence is that (QUOTE T) or (QUOTE X) is equivalent to T as a constant predicate.

The predicate eq has the following behavior.

1. If its arguments are different, the value of eq is NIL.

2. If its arguments are both the same atomic symbol, its value is *T*.

3. If its arguments are both the same, but are not atomic, then the value is *T* or NIL depending upon whether the arguments are identical in their representation in core memory.

4. The value of eq is always *T* or NIL. It is never undefined even if its arguments are bad.

23

IV. ARITHMETIC IN LISP

Lisp 1.5 has provision for handling fixed-point and floating-point numbers and logical words. There are functions and predicates in the system for performing arithmetic and logical operations and making basic tests.

4.1 Reading and Printing Numbers

Numbers are stored in the computer as though they were a special type of atomic symbol. This is discussed more thoroughly in section 7.3. The following points should be noted :

1. Numbers may occur in S-expressions as though they were atomic symbols.

2. Numbers are constants that evaluate to themselves. They do not need to be quoted.

3. Numbers should not be used as variables or function names.

a. Floating-Point Numbers

The rules for punching these for the read program are:

1. A decimal point must be included but not as the first or last character.

2. A plus sign or minus sign may precede the number. The plus sign is not required.

3. Exponent indication is optional. The letter E followed by the exponent to the base 10 is written directly after the number. The exponent consists of one or two digits that may be preceded by a plus or minus sign.

4. Absolute values must lie between 2^{128} and 2^{-128} (10^{38} and 10^{-38}).

5. Significance is limited to 8 decimal digits.

6. Any possible ambiguity between the decimal point and the point used in dot notation may be eliminated by putting spaces before and after the LISP dot. This is not required when there is no ambiguity.

Following are examples of correct floating-point numbers. These are all different forms for the same number, and will have the same effect when read in.

$$60.0$$
$$6.E1$$
$$600.00E-1$$
$$0.6E+2$$

The forms .6E+2 and 60. are incorrect because the decimal point is the first or last character respectively.

b. Fixed-Point Numbers

These are written as integers with an optional sign.

Examples

        −17
        32719

c. Octal Numbers or Logical Words

The correct form consists of

1. A sign (optional).
2. Up to 12 digits (0 through 7).
3. The letter Q.
4. An optional scale factor. The scale factor is a decimal integer, no sign allowed.

Example

  a. 777Q
  b. 777Q4
  c. –3Q11
  d. –7Q11
  e. +7Q11

The effect of the read program on octal numbers is as follows.

1. The number is placed in the accumulator three bits per octal digit with zeros added to the left-hand side to make twelve digits. The rightmost digit is placed in bits 33-35; the twelfth digit is placed in bits P, 1, and 2.

2. The accumulator is shifted left three bits (one octal digit) times the scale factor. Thus the scale factor is an exponent to the base 8.

3. If there is a negative sign, it is OR-ed into the P bit. The number is then stored as a logical word.

The examples a through e above will be converted to the following octal words. Note that because the sign is OR-ed with the 36th numerical bit c, d, and e are equivalent.

  a. 000000000777
  b. 000007770000
  c. 700000000000
  d. 700000000000
  e. 700000000000

4.2 Arithmetic Functions and Predicates

We shall now list all of the arithmetic functions in the System. They must be given numbers as arguments; otherwise an error condition will result. The arguments may be any type of number. A function may be given some fixed-point arguments and some floating-point arguments at the same time.

If all of the arguments for a function are fixed-point numbers, then the value will be a fixed-point number. If at least one argument is a floating-point number, then the value of the function will be a floating-point number.

plus$[x_1;\ldots;x_n]$ is a function of any number of arguments whose value is the algebraic sum of the arguments.

difference[x;y] has for its value the algebraic difference of its arguments.

minus[x] has for its value −x.

times[x_1;...;x_n] is a function of any number of arguments, whose value is the product (with correct sign) of its arguments.

add1[x] has x+1 for its value. The value is fixed-point or floating-point, depending on the argument.

sub1[x] has x−1 for its value. The value is fixed-point or floating-point, depending on the argument.

max[x_1;...;x_n] chooses the largest of its arguments for its value. Note that max[3;2.0] = 3.0.

min[x_1;...;x_n] chooses the smallest of its arguments for its value.

recip[x] computes 1/x. The reciprocal of any fixed point number is defined as zero.

quotient[x;y] computes the quotient of its arguments. For fixed-point arguments, the value is the number theoretic quotient. A divide check or floating-point trap will result in a LISP error.

remainder[x;y] computes the number theoretic remainder for fixed-point numbers, and the floating-point residue for floating-point arguments.

divide[x;y] = cons[quotient[x;y]; cons[remainder[x;y];NIL]]

expt[x;y] = x^y. If both x and y are fixed-point numbers, this is computed by iterative multiplication. Otherwise the power is computed by using logarithms. The first argument cannot be negative.

We shall now list all of the arithmetic predicates in the System. They may have fixed-point and floating-point arguments mixed freely. The value of a predicate is *T* or NIL.

lessp[x;y] is true if x < y, and false otherwise.

greaterp[x;y] is true if x > y.

zerop[x] is true if x=0, or if $|x| \leqslant 3 \times 10^{-6}$.

onep[x] is true if $|x-1| \leqslant 3 \times 10^{-6}$.

minusp[x] is true if x is negative.

          "−0" is negative.

numberp[x] is true if x is a number (fixed-point or floating-point).

fixp[x] is true only if x is a fixed-point number. If x is not a number at all, an error will result.

floatp[x] is similar to fixp[x] but for floating-point numbers.

equal[x;y] works on any arguments including S-expressions incorporating numbers inside them. Its value is true if the arguments are identical. Floating-point numbers must satisfy $|x-y| < 3 \times 10^{-6}$.

The logical functions operate on 36–bit words. The only acceptable arguments are fixed-point numbers. These may be read in as octal or decimal integers, or they may be the result of a previous computation.

logor[x_1;...;x_n] performs a logical OR on its arguments.

$\underline{\text{logand}}[x_1;\ldots;x_n]$ performs a logical AND on its arguments.

$\underline{\text{logxor}}[x_1;\ldots;x_n]$ performs an exclusive OR

$$(0 \underline{v} 0 = 0, \ 1 \underline{v} 0 = 0 \underline{v} 1 = 1, \ 1 \underline{v} 1 = 0).$$

$\underline{\text{leftshift}}[x;n] = x \times 2^n$. The first argument is shifted left by the number of bits specified by the second argument. If the second argument is negative, the first argument will be shifted right.

4.3 Programming with Arithmetic

The arithmetic functions may be used recursively, just as other functions available to the interpreter. As an example, we define $\underline{\text{factorial}}$ as it was given in Section I.

n! = [n = 0 →1; T →n.(n-1) !]
DEFINE ((
(FACTORIAL (LAMBDA (N) (COND
    ((ZEROP N) 1)
    (T (TIMES N (FACTORIAL (SUB1 N)))))))
))

4.4 The Array Feature

Provision is made in LISP 1.5 for allocating blocks of storage for data. The data may consist of numbers, atomic symbols or other S-expressions.

The pseudo-function $\underline{\text{array}}$ reserves space for arrays, and turns the name of an array into a function that can be used to fill the array or locate any element of it.

Arrays may have up to three indices. Each element (uniquely specified by its coordinates) contains a pointer to an S-expression (see Section VII).

$\underline{\text{array}}$ is a function of one argument which is a list of arrays to be declared. Each item is a list containing the name of an array, its dimensions, and the word LIST. (Non-list arrays are reserved for future developments of the LISP system.)

For example, to make an array called $\underline{\text{alpha}}$ of size 7 × 10, and one called $\underline{\text{beta}}$ of size 3 × 4 × 5 one should execute:

array[((ALPHA (7 10) LIST) (BETA (3 4 5) LIST))]

After this has been executed, both arrays exist and their elements are all set to NIL. Indices range from 0 to n-1.

$\underline{\text{alpha}}$ and $\underline{\text{beta}}$ are now functions that can be used to set or locate elements of these respective arrays.

To set $\text{alpha}_{i,j}$ to x, execute —

alpha[SET;x;i;j]

To set $\text{alpha}_{3,4}$ to (A B C) execute —

alpha[SET;(A B C);3;4]

Inside a function or program X might be bound to (A B C), I bound to 3, and J bound to 4, in which case the setting can be done by evaluating —

(ALPHA (QUOTE SET) X I J)

To locate an element of an array, use the array name as a function with the coordinates as axes. Thus any time after executing the previous example —

alpha[3;4] = (A B C)

Arrays use marginal indexing for maximum speed. For most efficient results, specify dimensions in increasing order. Beta[3;4;5] is better than beta[5;3;4].

Storage for arrays is located in an area of memory called binary program space.

V. THE PROGRAM FEATURE

The LISP 1.5 program feature allows the user to write an Algol-like program containing LISP statements to be executed.

An example of the program feature is the function <u>length</u>, which examines a list and decides how many elements there are in the top level of the list. The value of <u>length</u> is an integer.

<u>Length</u> is a function of one argument ℓ. The program uses two program variables <u>u</u> and <u>v</u>, which can be regarded as storage locations whose contents are to be changed by the program. In English the program is written:

> This is a function of one argument ℓ.
>
> > It is a program with two program variables <u>u</u> and <u>v</u>.
>
> Store 0 in <u>v</u>.
>
> Store the argument ℓ in <u>u</u>.

A   If <u>u</u> contains NIL, then the program is finished,

> > and the value is whatever is now in <u>v</u>.
>
> Store in <u>u</u>, <u>cdr</u> of what is now in <u>u</u>.
>
> Store in <u>v</u>, one more than what is now in <u>v</u>.
>
> Go to A.

We now write this program as an M-expression, with a few new notations. This corresponds line for line with the program written above.

$$\text{length}[\ell] = \text{prog}[[u;v];$$
$$v:=0;$$
$$u:=\ell;$$
$$\text{A}\qquad [\text{null}[u] \rightarrow \text{return}[v]];$$
$$u:= \text{cdr}[u];$$
$$v:= v+1;$$
$$\text{go } [A]]$$

Rewriting this as an S-expression, we get the following program.

```
DEFINE ((
(LENGTH (LAMBDA (L)
(PROG (U V)
        (SETQ V 0)
        (SETQ U L)
A       (COND ((NULL U) (RETURN V)))
        (SETQ U (CDR U))
        (SETQ V (ADD1 V))
        (GO A) )))        ))
LENGTH ((A  B  C  D))
```

The last two lines are test cases. Their values are four and five, respectively.

The program form has the structure —

(PROG, list of program variables, sequence of statements and atomic symbols...)
An atomic symbol in the list is the location marker for the statement that follows. In the above example, A is a location marker for the statement beginning with COND.

The first list after the symbol PROG is a list of program variables. If there are none, then this should be written NIL or (). Program variables are treated much like bound variables, but they are not bound by LAMBDA. The value of each program variable is NIL until it has been set to something else.

To set a program variable, use the form SET. To set variable PI to 3.14 write (SET (QUOTE PI) 3.14). SETQ is like SET except that it quotes its first argument. Thus (SETQ PI 3.14). SETQ is usually more convenient. SET and SETQ can change variables that are on the a-list from higher level functions. The value of SET or SETQ is the value of its second argument.

Statements are normally executed in sequence. Executing a statement means evaluating it with the current a-list and ignoring its value. Program statements are often executed for their effect rather than their value.

GO is a form used to cause a transfer. (GO A) will cause the program to continue at statement A. The form GO can be used only as a statement on the top level of a PROG or immediately inside a COND which is on the top level of a PROG.

Conditional expressions as program statements have a useful peculiarity. If none of the propositions are true, instead of an error indication which would otherwise occur, the program continues with the next statement. This is true only for conditional expressions that are on the top level of a PROG.

RETURN is the normal end of a program. The argument of RETURN is evaluated, and this is the value of the program. No further statements are executed.

If a program runs out of statements, it returns with the value NIL.

The program feature, like other LISP functions, can be used recursively. The function <u>rev</u>, which reverses a list and all its sublists is an example of this.

$$rev[x] = prog[[y;z];$$
$$A \quad [null[x] \rightarrow return[y];$$
$$z := car[x];$$
$$[atom[z] \rightarrow go[B]];$$
$$z := rev[z];$$
$$B \quad y := cons[z;y];$$
$$x := cdr[x];$$
$$go[A]]$$

The function <u>rev</u> will reverse a list on all levels so that
$$rev[(A ((B C) D))] = ((D (C B)) A)$$

VI. RUNNING THE LISP SYSTEM

6.1 Preparing a Card Deck

A LISP program consists of several sections called packets. Each packet starts with an Overlord direction card, followed by a set of doublets for <u>evalquote,</u> and ending with the word STOP.

Overlord direction cards control tape movement, restoration of the system memory between packets, and core dumps. A complete listing of Overlord directions is given in Appendix E.

Overlord direction cards are punched in Share symbolic format; the direction starts in column 8, and the comments field starts in column 16. Some Overlord cards will now be described.

<u>TEST</u>: Subsequent doublets are read in until the word STOP is encountered, or until a read error occurs. The doublets are then evaluated and each doublet with its value is written on the output tape. If an error occurs, a diagnostic will be written and the program will continue with the next doublet. When all doublets have been evaluated, control is returned to Overlord which restores the core memory to what it was before the TEST by reading in a core memory image from the temporary tape.

<u>SET</u>: The doublets are read and interpreted in the same manner as a TEST. However, when all doublets have been evaluated, the core memory is not restored. Instead, the core memory is written out onto the temporary tape (overwriting the previous core image), and becomes the base memory for all remaining packets. Definitions and other memory changes made during a SET will affect all remaining packets.

Several SET's during a LISP run will set on top of each other.

A SET will not set if it contains an error. The memory will be restored from the temporary tape instead.

<u>SETSET</u>: This direction is like SET, except that it will set even if there is an error.

<u>FIN</u>: End of LISP run.

The reading of doublets is normally terminated by the word STOP. If parentheses do not count out, STOP will appear to be inside an S-expression and will not be recognized as such. To prevent reading from continuing indefinitely, each packet should end with STOP followed by a large number of right parentheses. An unpaired right parenthesis will cause a read error and terminate reading.

A complete card deck for a LISP run might consist of:

      a: LISP loader

      b: ID card (Optional)

      c: Several Packets

      d: FIN card

      e: Two blank cards to prevent card reader from hanging up

The ID card may have any information desired by the computation center. It will be printed at the head of the output.

6.2 Tracing

Tracing is a technique used to debug recursive functions. The tracer prints the name of a function and its arguments when it is entered, and its value when it is finished. By tracing certain critical subfunctions, the user can often locate a fault in a large program.

Tracing is controlled by the pseudo-function trace, whose argument is a list of functions to be traced. After trace has been executed, tracing will occur whenever these functions are entered.

When tracing of certain functions is no longer desired, it can be terminated by the pseudo-function untrace whose argument is a list of functions that are no longer to be traced.

6.3 Error Diagnostics

When an error occurs in a LISP 1.5 program, a diagnostic giving the nature of the error is printed out. The diagnostic gives the type of error, and the contents of certain registers at that time. In some cases a back-trace is also printed. This is a list of functions that were entered recursively but not completed at the time of the error.

In most cases, the program continues with the next doublet. However, certain errors are fatal; in this case control is given to the monitor Overlord. Errors during Overlord also continue with Overlord.

A complete list of error diagnostics is given below, with comments.

Interpreter Errors:

A 1	APPLIED FUNCTION CALLED ERROR	

The function error will cause an error diagnostic to occur. The argument (if any) of error will be printed. Error is of some use as a debugging aid.

A 2   FUNCTION OBJECT HAS NO DEFINITION— APPLY

This occurs when an atomic symbol, given as the first argument of apply, does not have a definition either on its property list or on the a-list of apply.

A 3   CONDITIONAL UNSATISFIED — EVCON

None of the propostiions following COND are true.

A 4   SETQ GIVEN ON NONEXISTENT PROGRAM VARIABLE — APPLY

A 5   SET GIVEN ON NONEXISTENT PROGRAM VARIABLE — APPLY

A 6   GO REFERS TO A POINT NOT LABELLED — INTER

A 7   TOO MANY ARGUMENTS — SPREAD

The interpreter can handle only 20 arguments for a function.

A 8   UNBOUND VARIABLE — EVAL

The atomic symbol in question is not bound on the a-list for eval nor does it have an APVAL.

A 9　　　FUNCTION OBJECT HAS NO DEFINITION – EVAL

Eval expects the first object on a list to be evaluated to be an atomic symbol. A 8 and A 9 frequently occur when a parenthesis miscount causes the wrong phrase to be evaluated.

Compiler Errors:

C 1　　　CONDITION NOT SATISFIED IN COMPILED FUNCTION

Character-Handling Functions:

CH 1　　TOO MANY CHARACTERS IN PRINT NAME – PACK

CH 2　　FLOATING POINT NUMBER OUT OF RANGE – NUMOB

CH 3　　TAPE READING ERROR – ADVANCE

The character-handling functions are described in Appendix F.

Miscellaneous Errors:

F 1　　　CONS COUNTER TRAP

The cons counter is described in section 6.4.

F 2　　　FIRST ARGUMENT LIST TOO SHORT – PAIR

F 3　　　SECOND ARGUMENT LIST TOO SHORT – PAIR

Pair is used by the interpreter to bind variables to arguments. If a function is given the wrong number of arguments, these errors may occur.

F 5　　　STR TRAP – CONTINUING WITH NEXT EVALQUOTE

When the instruction STR is executed, this error occurs. If sense switch 6 is down when an STR is executed, control goes to Overlord instead.

G 1　　　FLOATING POINT TRAP OR DIVIDE CHECK

G 2　　　OUT OF PUSH – DOWN LIST

The push-down list is the memory device that keeps track of the level of recursion. When recursion becomes very deep, this error will occur. Non-terminating recursion will cause this error.

Garbage Collector Errors:

GC 1　　FATAL ERROR – RECLAIMER

This error only occurs when the system is so choked that it cannot be restored. Control goes to Overlord.

GC 2　　NOT ENOUGH WORDS COLLECTED – RECLAIMER

This error restores free storage as best it can and continues with the next doublet.

Arithmetic Errors:

I 1　　　NOT ENOUGH ROOM FOR ARRAY

Arrays are stored in binary program space.

I 2   FIRST ARGUMENT NEGATIVE – EXPT
I 3   BAD ARGUMENT – NUMVAL
I 4   BAD ARGUMENT – FIXVAL
        Errors I 3 and I 4 will occur when numerical functions are given wrong arguments.

Lap Errors:
L 1   UNABLE TO DETERMINE ORIGIN
L 2   OUT OF BINARY PROGRAM SPACE
L 3   UNDEFINED SYMBOL
L 4   FIELD CONTAINED SUB – SUBFIELDS

Overlord Errors:
O 1   ERROR IN SIZE CARD – OVERLORD
O 2   INVALID TAPE DESIGNATION – OVERLORD
O 3   NO SIZE CARD – OVERLORD
O 4   BAD DUMP ARGUMENTS – OVERLORD
O 5   BAD INPUT BUT GOING ON ANYHOW – OVERLORD
O 7   OVERLAPPING PARAMETERS – SETUP

Input-Output Errors:
P 1   PRIN1 ASKED TO PRINT NON-OBJECT
R 1   FIRST OBJECT ON INPUT LIST IS ILLEGAL – RDA
        This error occurs when the read program encounters a character such as
        ")" or "." out of context. This occurs frequently when there is a parenthesis
        miscount.
R 2   CONTEXT ERROR WITH DOT NOTATION – RDA
R 3   ILLEGAL CHARACTER – RDA
R 4   END OF FILE ON READ-IN – RDA
R 5   PRINT NAME TOO LONG – RDA
        Print names may contain up to 30 BCD characters.
R 6   NUMBER TOO LARGE IN CONVERSION – RDA

6.4 The Cons Counter and Errorset

The cons counter is a useful device for breaking out of program loops. It automatically causes a trap when a certain number of conses have been performed.

The counter is turned on by executing count [n], where n is an integer. If n conses are performed before the counter is turned off, a trap will occur and an error diagnostic will be given. The counter is turned off by uncount [NIL]. The counter is turned on and reset each time count [n] is executed. The counter can be turned on so as to continue counting from the state it was in when last turned off by executing count [NIL].

The function speak [NIL] gives the number of conses counted since the counter was last reset.

34

errorset is a function available to the interpreter and compiler for making a graceful retreat from an error condition encountered during a subroutine.

errorset[e;n;m;a] is a pseudo-function with four arguments. If no error occurs, then errorset can be defined by

errorset[e;n;m;a] = list[eval[e;a]]

n is the number of conses permitted before a cons trap will occur. The cons counter is always on during an errorset; however, when leaving the errorset the counter is always restored to the value it had before entering the errorset. The on-off status of the counter will also be restored.

When an error occurs inside an errorset, the error diagnostic will occur if m is set true, but will not be printed if m is NIL.

If an error occurs inside of an errorset, then the value of errorset is NIL. If variables bound outside of the errorset have not been altered by using cset or set, and if no damage has been done by pseudo-functions, it may be possible to continue computation in a different direction when one path results in an error.

VII. LIST STRUCTURES

In other sections of this manual, lists have been discussed by using the LISP input-output language. In this section, we discuss the representation of lists inside the computer, the nature of property lists of atomic symbols, representation of numbers, and the garbage collector.

7.1 Representation of List Structure

Lists are not stored in the computer as sequences of BCD characters, but as structural forms built out of computer words as parts of trees.

In representing list structure, a computer word will be depicted as a rectangle divided into two sections, the address and decrement.

Each of these is a 15-bit field of the word.

We define a pointer to a computer word as the 15-bit quantity that is the complement of the address of the word. Thus a pointer to location 77777 would be 00001.

Suppose the decrement of word x contains a pointer to word y. We diagram this as

We can now give a rule for representing S-expressions in the computer. The representation of atomic symbols will be explained in section 7.3. When a computer word contains a pointer to an atomic symbol in the address or decrement, the atomic symbol will be written there as

ONION

The rule for representing non-atomic S-expressions is to start with a word containing a pointer to <u>car</u> of the expression in the address, and a pointer to <u>cdr</u> of the expression in the decrement.

Following are some diagrammed S-expressions, shown as they would appear in the computer. It is convenient to indicate NIL by ▱ instead of NIL .

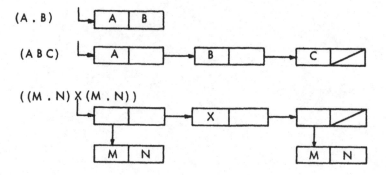

It is possible for lists to make use of common subexpressions. ((M . N) X (M . N)) could also be represented as

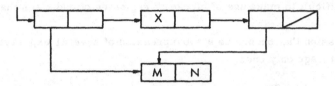

Circular lists are ordinarily not permitted. They may not be read in; however, they can occur inside the computer as the result of computations involving certain functions. Their printed representation is infinite in length. For example, the structure

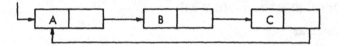

will print as (A B C A B C A...

That which follows is an actual assembly listing of the S-expression (A (B (C . A)) (C . A)) which is diagrammed:

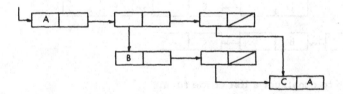

The atoms A, B, and C are represented by pointers to locations 12327, 12330, and 12331, respectively. NIL is represented by a pointer to location 00000.

10425	0 67352 0 65451	−A, , −*−1
10426	0 67351 0 67350	−*−2, , −*−1
10427	0 00000 0 67346	−*−3
10430	0 67347 0 65450	−B, , −*−1
10431	0 00000 0 67346	−*−1
10432	0 65451 0 65447	−C, , −A

The advantages of list structures for the storage of symbolic expressions are:

1. The size and even the number of expressions with which the program will have to deal cannot be predicted in advance. Therefore, it is difficult to arrange blocks of

storage of fixed length to contain them.

2. Registers can be put back on the free-storage list when they are no longer needed. Even one register returned to the list is of value, but if expressions are stored linearly, it is difficult to make use of blocks of registers of odd sizes that may become available.

3. An expression that occurs as a subexpression of several expressions need be represented in storage only once.

7.2 Construction of List Structure

The following simple example has been included to illustrate the exact construction of list structures. Two types of list structures are shown, and a function for deriving one from the other is given in LISP.

We assume that we have a list of the form

$$\ell_1 = ((A\ B\ C)\ (D\ E\ F), \ldots, (X\ Y\ Z)),$$

which is represented as

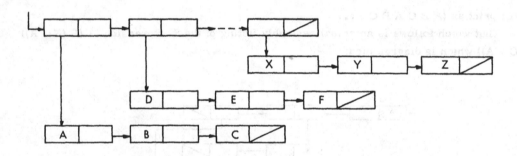

and that we wish to construct a list of the form

$$\ell_2 = ((A\ (B\ C))\ (D\ (E\ F)), \ldots, (X\ (Y\ Z)))$$

which is represented as

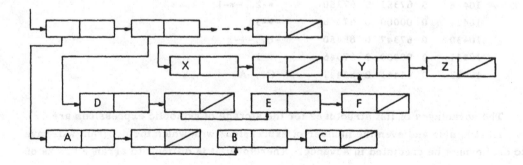

We consider the typical substructure, (A (B C)) of the second list ℓ_2. This may be constructed from A, B, and C by the operation

cons[A;cons[cons[B;cons[C;NIL]];NIL]]

or, using the <u>list</u> function, we can write the same thing as

list[A;list[B;C]]

In any case, given a list, x, of three atomic symbols,

x = (A B C),

the arguments A, B, and C to be used in the previous construction are found from

A = car[x]

B = cadr[x]

C = caddr[x]

The first step in obtaining ℓ_2 from ℓ_1 is to define a function, <u>grp</u>, of three arguments which creates (X (Y Z)) from a list of the form (X Y Z).

grp[x] = list[car[x];list[cadr[x];caddr[x]]]

Then <u>grp</u> is used on the list ℓ_1, under the assumption that ℓ_1 is of the form given. For this purpose, a new function, mltgrp, is defined as

mltgrp[ℓ] = [null[ℓ] → NIL;T → cons[grp[car[ℓ]];mltgrp[cdr[ℓ]]]]

So <u>mltgrp</u> applied to the list ℓ_1 takes each threesome, (X Y Z), in turn and applies <u>grp</u> to it to put it in the new form, (X (Y Z)) until the list ℓ_1 has been exhausted and the new list ℓ_2 achieved.

7.3 Property Lists

In other sections, atomic symbols have been considered only as pointers. In this section the property lists of atomic symbols that begin at the appointed locations are described.

Every atomic symbol has a property list. When an atomic symbol is read in for the first time, a property list is created for it.

A property list is characterized by having the special constant 77777_8 (i.e., minus 1) as the first element of the list. The rest of the list contains various properties of the atomic symbol. Each property is preceded by an atomic symbol which is called its indicator. Some of the indicators are:

PNAME   – the BCD print name of the atomic symbol for input-output use.

EXPR   – S-expression defining a function whose name is the atomic symbol on whose property list the EXPR appears.

SUBR   – Function defined by a machine language subroutine.

APVAL   – Permanent value for the atomic symbol considered as a variable.

The atomic symbol NIL has two things on its property list – its PNAME, and an APVAL that gives it a value of NIL. Its property list looks like this:

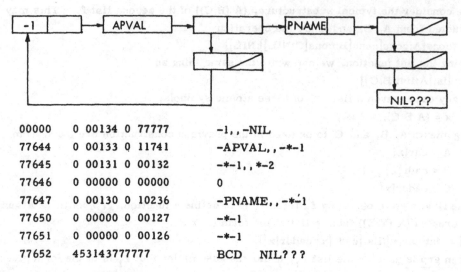

```
00000    0 00134 0 77777        -1,,-NIL
77644    0 00133 Q 11741        -APVAL,,-*-1
77645    0 00131 0 00132        -*-1,,*-2
77646    0 00000 0 00000        0
77647    0 00130 0 10236        -PNAME,,-*-1
77650    0 00000 0 00127        -*-1
77651    0 00000 0 00126        -*-1
77652    453143777777           BCD    NIL???
```

The print name (PNAME) is depressed two levels to allow for names of more than six BCD characters. The last word of the print name is filled out with the illegal BCD character 77_8 (?). The print name of EXAMPLE would look like this:

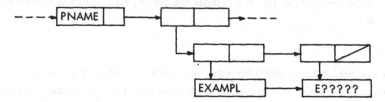

The property list of a machine-language function contains the indicator SUBR followed by a TXL instruction giving the location of the subroutine and the number of arguments. For example

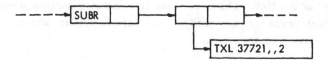

The indicator EXPR points to an S-expression defining a function. The function define puts EXPR's on property lists. After defining ff, its property list would look like this

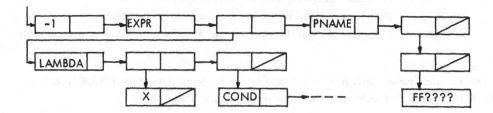

40

The function get[x;i] can be used to find a property of x whose indicator is i. The value of get[FF;EXPR] would be (LAMBDA (X) (COND...

A property with its indicator can be removed by remprop[x;i].

The function deflist[x;i] can be used to put any indicator on a property list. The first argument is a list of pairs as for define, the second argument is the indicator to be used. define[x] = deflist[x;EXPR].

An indicator on a property list that does not have a property following it is called a flag. For example, the flag TRACE is a signal that a function is to be traced. Flags can be put on property lists and removed by using the pseudo-functions flag and remflag.

Numbers are represented by a type of atomic symbol in LISP. This word consists of a word with -1 in the address, certain bits in the tag which specify that it is a number and what type it is, and a pointer to the number itself in the decrement of this word.

Unlike atomic symbols, numbers are not stored uniquely.

For example, the decimal number 15 is represented as follows:

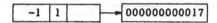

7.4 List Structure Operators

The theory of recursive functions developed in Section I will be referred to as elementary LISP. Although this language is universal in terms of computable functions of symbolic expressions, it is not convenient as a programming system without additional tools to increase its power.

In particular, elementary LISP has no ability to modify list structure. The only basic function that affects list structure is cons, and this does not change existing lists, but creates new lists. Functions written in pure LISP such as subst do not actually modify their arguments, but make the modifications while copying the original.

LISP is made general in terms of list structure by means of the basic list operators rplaca and rplacd. These operators can be used to replace the address or decrement or any word in a list. They are used for their effect, as well as for their value, and are called pseudo-functions.

rplaca[x;y] replaces the address of x with y. Its value is x, but x is something different from what it was before. In terms of value, rplaca can be described by the equation

rplaca[x;y] = cons[y;cdr[x]]

But the effect is quite different: there is no cons involved and a new word is not created.

rplacd[x;y] replaces the decrement of x with y.

These operators must be used with caution. They can permanently alter existing definitions and other basic memory. They can be used to create circular lists, which can cause infinite printing, and look infinite to functions that search, such as equal and subst.

As an example, consider the function mltgrp of section 7.2. This is a list-altering

41

function that alters a copy of its argument. The subfunction <u>grp</u> rearranges a subgroup

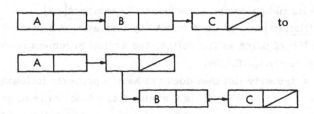

to

The original function does this by creating new list structures, and uses four <u>cons</u>'s.
Because there are only three words in the original, at least one <u>cons</u> is necessary, but
<u>grp</u> can be rewritten by using <u>rplaca</u> and <u>rplacd</u>.

The modification is

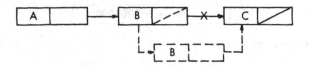

The new word is created by cons[cadr[x];cddr[x]]. A pointer to it is provided by
rplaca[cdr[x];cons[cadr[x];cddr[x]]].

The other modification is to break the pointer from the second to the third word.
This is done by rplacd[cdr[x];NIL].

<u>pgrp</u> is now defined as

pgrp[x] = rplacd[rplaca[cdr[x];cons[cadr[x];cddr[x]]];NIL]

The function <u>pgrp</u> is used entirely for its effect. Its value is not useful, being the
substructure ((B C)). Therefore a new <u>mltgrp</u> is needed that executes <u>pgrp</u> and ignores
its value. Since the top level is not to be copied, <u>mltgrp</u> should do no <u>consing</u>.

pmltgrp[ℓ] = [null[ℓ] → NIL;

T → prog2[pgrp[car[ℓ]];pmltgrp[cdr[ℓ]]]]

<u>prog2</u> is a function that evaluates its two arguments. Its value is the second argument.

The value of <u>pmltgrp</u> is NIL. <u>pgrp</u> and <u>pmltgrp</u> are pseudo-functions.

7.5 The Free-Storage List and the Garbage Collector

At any given time only a part of the memory reserved for list structures will actually
be in use for storing S-expressions. The remaining registers are arranged in a single
list called the <u>free-storage list</u>. A certain register, FREE, in the program contains the
location of the first register in this list. When a word is required to form some additional list structure, the first word on the <u>free-storage list</u> is taken and the number in
register FREE is changed to become the location of the second word on the free-storage

42

list. No provision need be made for the user to program the return of registers to the free-storage list.

This return takes place automatically whenever the free-storage list has been exhausted during the running of a LISP program. The program that retrieves the storage is called the garbage collector.

Any piece of list structure that is accessible to programs in the machine is considered an active list and is not touched by the garbage collector. The active lists are accessible to the program through certain fixed sets of base registers, such as the registers in the list of atomic symbols, the registers that contain partial results of the LISP computation in progress, etc. The list structures involved may be arbitrarily long but each register that is active must be connected to a base register through a car-cdr chain of registers. Any register that cannot be so reached is not accessible to any program and is nonactive; therefore its contents are no longer of interest.

The nonactive, i.e., inaccessible, registers are reclaimed for the free-storage list by the garbage collector as follows. First, every active register that can be reached through a car-cdr chain is marked by setting its sign negative. Whenever a negative register is reached in a chain during this process, the garbage collector knows that the rest of the list involving that register has already been marked. Then the garbage collector does a linear sweep of the free-storage area, collecting all registers with a positive sign into a new free-storage list, and restoring the original signs of the active registers.

Sometimes list structure points to full words such as BCD print names and numbers. The garbage collector cannot mark these words because the sign bit may be in use. The garbage collector must also stop tracing because the pointers in the address and decrement of a full word are not meaningful.

These problems are solved by putting full words in a reserved section of memory called full-word space. The garbage collector stops tracing as soon as it leaves the free-storage space. Marking in full-word space is accomplished by a bit table.

VIII. A COMPLETE LISP PROGRAM — THE WANG ALGORITHM FOR THE PROPOSITIONAL CALCULUS

This section gives an example of a complete collection of LISP function definitions which were written to define an algorithm. The program was then run on several test cases. The algorithm itself is explained, and is then written in M-expressions. The complete input card deck and the printed output of the run are reprinted here.

The Wang Algorithm[1] is a method of deciding whether or not a formula in the propositional calculus is a theorem. The reader will need to know something about the propositional calculus in order to understand this discussion.

We quote from pages 5 and 6 of Wang's paper:

"The propositional calculus (System P)

Since we are concerned with practical feasibility, it is preferable to use more logical connectives to begin with when we wish actually to apply the procedure to concrete cases. For this purpose we use the five usual logical constants $\sim$ (not), $\&$ (conjunction), $\lor$ (disjunction), $\supset$ (implication), $\equiv$ (biconditional), with their usual interpretations.

"A propositional letter P, Q, R, M or N, et cetera, is a formula (and an "atomic formula"). If ϕ, ψ are formulae, then $\sim\phi$, $\phi \& \psi$, $\phi \lor \psi$, $\phi \supset \psi$, $\phi \equiv \psi$ are formulae. If π, ρ are strings of formulae (each, in particular, might be an empty string or a single formula) and ϕ is a formula, then π, ϕ, ρ is a string and $\pi \rightarrow \rho$ is a sequent which, intuitively speaking, is true if and only if either some formula in the string π (the "antecedent") is false or some formula in the string ρ (the "consequent") is true, i.e., the conjunction of all formulae in the antecedent implies the disjunction of all formulae in the consequent.

"There are eleven rules of derivation. An initial rule states that a sequent with only atomic formulae (proposition letters) is a theorem if and only if a same formula occurs on both sides of the arrow. There are two rules for each of the five truth functions — one introducing it into the antecedent, one introducing it into the consequent. One need only reflect on the intuitive meaning of the truth functions and the arrow sign to be convinced that these rules are indeed correct. Later on, a proof will be given of their completeness, i.e., all intuitively valid sequents are provable, and of their consistency, i.e., all provable sequents are intuitively valid.

"P1. Initial rule: if λ, ζ are strings of atomic formulae, then $\lambda \rightarrow \zeta$ is a theorem if some atomic formula occurs on both sides of the arrow.

"In the ten rules listed below, λ and ζ are always strings (possibly empty) of atomic formulae. As a proof procedure in the usual sense, each proof begins with a finite set of cases of P1 and continues with successive consequences obtained by the other rules."

---

1. Wang, Hao. "Toward Mechanical Mathematics," IBM J. Res. Develop., Vol.4, No. 1. January 1960.

"As will be explained below, a proof looks like a tree structure growing in the wrong direction. We shall, however, be chiefly interested in doing the step backwards, thereby incorporating the process of searching for a proof.

"The rules are so designed that given any sequent, we can find the first logical connective, and apply the appropriate rule to eliminate it, thereby resulting in one or two premises which, taken together, are equivalent to the conclusion. This process can be repeated until we reach a finite set of sequents with atomic formulae only. Each connective-free sequent can then be tested for being a theorem or not, by the initial rule. If all of them are theorems, then the original sequent is a theorem and we obtain a proof; otherwise we get a counterexample and a disproof. Some simple samples will make this clear.

"For example, given any theorem of "Principia," we can automatically prefix an arrow to it and apply the rules to look for a proof. When the main connective is $\supset$, it is simpler, though not necessary, to replace the main connective by an arrow and proceed. For example:

*2.45. $\vdash\!\!-\!\!-: \sim (P \vee Q) . \supset . \sim P$,
*5.21. $\vdash\!\!-\!\!-: \sim P \,\&\sim Q . \supset . P \equiv Q$

can be rewritten and proved as follows:

*2.45. $\sim (P \vee Q) \rightarrow \sim P$

    (1) $\rightarrow \sim P, \; P \vee Q$

    (2) $P \rightarrow P \vee Q$

    (3) $P \rightarrow P, Q$

    VALID

*5.21. $\rightarrow \sim P \,\& \sim Q . \supset . P \equiv Q$

    (1) $\sim P \,\&\sim Q \rightarrow P \equiv Q$

    (2) $\sim P, \; \sim Q \rightarrow P \equiv Q$

    (3) $\sim Q \rightarrow P \equiv Q, P$

    (4) $\rightarrow P \equiv Q, P, Q$

    (5) $P \rightarrow Q, P, Q$

    VALID

    (5) $Q \rightarrow P, P, Q$

    VALID

P2a. Rule $\rightarrow \sim$: If $\phi, \; \zeta \rightarrow \lambda, \rho$, then $\zeta \rightarrow \lambda, \sim \phi, \rho$.

P2b. Rule $\sim \rightarrow$: If $\lambda, \rho \rightarrow \pi, \phi$, then $\lambda, \sim \phi, \; \rho \rightarrow \pi$.

P3a. Rule $\rightarrow \&$: If $\zeta \rightarrow \lambda, \phi, \; \rho$ and $\zeta \rightarrow \lambda, \psi, \rho$, then $\zeta \rightarrow \lambda, \phi \& \psi, \rho$.

P3b. Rule $\& \rightarrow$: If $\lambda, \phi, \psi, \rho \rightarrow \pi$, then $\lambda, \phi \& \psi, \; \rho \rightarrow \pi$.

P4a. Rule $\rightarrow \vee$: If $\zeta \rightarrow \lambda, \phi, \psi, \rho$, then $\zeta \rightarrow \lambda, \phi \vee \psi, \rho$.

P4b. Rule $\vee \rightarrow$: If $\lambda, \phi, \; \rho \rightarrow \pi$ and $\lambda, \psi, \; \rho \rightarrow \pi$, then $\lambda, \phi \vee \psi, \; \rho \rightarrow \pi$.

P5a. Rule $\rightarrow \supset$: If $\zeta, \phi \rightarrow \lambda, \psi, \rho$, then $\zeta \rightarrow \lambda, \phi \supset \psi, \rho$.

P5b.   Rule ⊃ → :   If λ, ψ, ρ → π and λ, ρ → π, φ, then λ, φ⊃ψ, ρ → π .

P6a.   Rule → ≡ :   If φ, ζ → λ, ψ, ρ and ψ, ζ → λ, φ, ρ , then ζ → λ, φ≡ψ, ρ .

P6b.   Rule ≡ → :   If φ, ψ, λ, ρ → π and λ, ρ → π, φ, ψ, then λ, φ ≡ ψ, ρ → π ."

(2)   **The LISP Program**.   We define a function theorem[s] whose value is truth or falsity according to whether the sequent s is theorem.

The sequent

$$s: \phi_1, \dots, \phi_n \to \psi_1, \dots, \psi_m$$

is represented by the S-expression

$$s^*: (ARROW, (\phi_1^*, \dots, \phi_n^*), (\psi_1^*, \dots, \psi_m^*))$$

where in each case the ellipsis ... denotes missing terms, and where ϕ^* denotes the S-expression for ϕ.

Propositional formulae are represented as follows:

1.   For "atomic formulae" (Wang's terminology) we use "atomic symbols" (LISP terminology).

2.   The following table gives our "Cambridge Polish" way of representing propositional formulae with given main connectives.

1. ~ φ	becomes	(NOT φ*)
2. φ & ψ	becomes	(AND φ* ψ*)
3. φ ∨ ψ	becomes	(OR φ* ψ*)
4. φ ⊃ ψ	becomes	(IMPLIES φ* ψ*)
5. φ ≡ ψ	becomes	(EQUIV φ* ψ*)

Thus the sequent

$$\sim P \, \& \sim Q \to P \equiv Q, R \lor S$$

is represented by

(ARROW ((AND (NOT P) (NOT Q))) ((EQUIV P Q) (OR R S)))

The S-function theorem[s] is given in terms of auxiliary functions as follows:

theorem[s] = th1[NIL;NIL;cadr[s] ;caddr[s]]

th1[a1;a2;a;c] = [null[a] → th2[a1;a2;NIL;NIL;c];T →
    member[car[a];c] ∨ [atom[car[a]] →
    th1[[member[car[a];a1] → a1;T → cons[car[
    a];a1]];a2;cdr[a];c];T → th1[a1;[
    member[car[a];a2] → a2;T → cons[
    car[a];a2]];cdr[a];c]]]

th2[a1;a2;c1;c2;c] = [null[c] → th[a1;a2;c1;c2];atom[
    car[c]] → th2[a1;a2;[member[car[
    c];c1] → c1;T → cons[car[c];c1]];

46

$$c2;cdr[c]];T \to th2[a1;a2;c1;[$$
$$member[car[c];c2] \to c2;T \to cons[$$
$$car[c];c2]];cdr[c]]]$$

$$th[a1;a2;c1;c2] = [null[a2] \to \sim null[c2] \wedge thr[car[c2];$$
$$a1;a2;c1;cdr[c2]];T \to th\ell[car[a2];$$
$$a1;cdr[a2];c1;c2]]$$

<u>th</u> is the main predicate through which all the recursions take place. <u>theorem</u>, <u>th1</u> and <u>th2</u> break up and sort the information in the sequent for the benefit of <u>th</u>. The four arguments of <u>th</u> are:

 a1: atomic formulae on left side of arrow
 a2: other formulae on left side of arrow
 c1: atomic formulae on right side of arrow
 c2: other formulae on right side of arrow

 The atomic formulae are kept separate from the others in order to make faster the detection of the occurrence of formula on both sides of the arrow and the finding of the next formula to reduce. Each use of <u>th</u> represents one reduction according to one of the 10 rules. The forumla to be reduced is chosen from the left side of the arrow if possible. According to whether the formula to be reduced is on the left or right we use <u>thℓ</u> or <u>thr</u>. We have

$$th\ell[u;a1;a2;c1;c2] = [$$
$$car[u] = NOT \to th1r[cadr[u];a1;a2;c1;c2];$$
$$car[u] = AND \to th2\ell[cdr[u];a1;a2;c1;c2];$$
$$car[u] = OR \to th1\ell[cadr[u];a1;a2;c1;c2] \wedge th1\ell$$
$$caddr[u];a1;a2;c1;c2];$$
$$car[u] = IMPLIES \to th1\ell[caddr[u];a1;a2;c1;c2] \wedge th1r$$
$$cadr[u];a1;a2;c1;c2];$$
$$car[u] = EQUIV \to th2\ell[cdr[u];a1;a2;c1;c2] \wedge th2r$$
$$cdr[u];a1;a2;c1;c2];$$
$$T \to error[list[THL;u;a1;a2;c1;c2]]]$$

$$thr[u;a1;a2;c1;c2] = [$$
$$car[u] = NOT \to th1\ell[cadr[u];a1;a2;c1;c2];$$
$$car[u] = AND \to th1r[cadr[u];a1;a2;c1;c2] \wedge th1r$$
$$caddr[u];a1;a2;c1;c2];$$
$$car[u] = OR \to th2r[cdr[u];a1;a2;c1;c2];$$
$$car[u] = IMPLIES \to th11[cadr[u];caddr[u];a1;a2;c1;c2];$$
$$car[u] = EQUIV \to th11[cadr[u];caddr[u];a1;a2;c1;c2] \wedge$$
$$th11[caddr[u];cadr[u];a1;a2;c1;c2];$$
$$T \to error[THR;u;a1;a2;c1;c2]]]$$

The functions th1ℓ, th1r, th2ℓ, th2r, th11 distribute the parts of the reduced formula to the appropriate places in the reduced sequent.

These functions are

th1ℓ[v;a1;a2;c1;c2] = [atom[v] → member[v;c1] ∨
   th[cons[v;a1];a1;c1;c2];T → member[v;c2] ∨
   th[a1;cons[v;a2];c1;c2]]

th1r[v;a1;a2;c1;c2] = [atom[v] → member[v;a1] ∨
   th[a1;a2;cons[v;c1];c2];T → member[v;a2] ∨
   th[a1;a2;c1;cons[v;c2]]]

th2ℓ[v;a1;a2;c1;c2] = [atom[car[v]] → member[car[v];c1] ∨
   th1ℓ[cadr[v];cons[car[v];a1];a2;c1;c2];T → member[
     car[v];c2] ∨
   th1ℓ[cadr[v];a1;cons[car[v];a2];c1;c2]]

th2r[v;a1;a2;c1;c2] = [atom[car[v]] → member[car[v];a1] ∨
   th1r[cadr[v];a1;a2;cons[car[v];c1];c2];T → member[∨
     car[v];a2] ∨
   th1r[cadr[v];a1;a2;c1;cons[car[v];c2]]]

th11[v1;v2;a1;a2;c1;c2] = [atom[v1] → member[v1;c1] ∨
   th1r[v2;cons[v1;a1];a2;c1;c2];T → member[v1;c2] ∨
   th1r[v2;a1;cons[v1;a2];c1;c2]]

Finally the function member is defined by

member[x;u] = ~null[u] ∧ [equal[x;car[u]] ∨ member[x;cdr[u]]]

The entire card deck is reprinted below, with only the two loader cards, which are binary, omitted. The function member is not defined because it is already in the system.

* M948-1207 LEVIN, LISP, TEST, 2, 3, 250, 0
    TEST   WANG ALGORITHM FOR THE PROPOSITIONAL CALCULUS

DEFINE((
(THEOREM (LAMBDA (S) (TH1 NIL NIL (CADR S) (CADDR S))))

```
(TH1 (LAMBDA (A1 A2 A C) (COND ((NULL A)
    (TH2 A1 A2 NIL NIL C)) (T
    (OR (MEMBER (CAR A) C) (COND ((ATOM (CAR A))
    (TH1 (COND ((MEMBER (CAR A) A1) A1)
    (T (CONS (CAR A) A1))) A2 (CDR A) C))
    (T (TH1 A1 (COND ((MEMBER (CAR A) A2) A2)
    (T (CONS (CAR A) A2))) (CDR A) C)))))))

(TH2 (LAMBDA (A1 A2 C1 C2 C) (COND
    ((NULL C) (TH A1 A2 C1 C2))
    ((ATOM (CAR C)) (TH2 A1 A2 (COND
    ((MEMBER (CAR C) C1) C1) (T
    (CONS (CAR C) C1))) C2 (CDR C)))
    (T (TH2 A1 A2 C1 (COND ((MEMBER
    (CAR C) C2) C2) (T (CONS (CAR C) C2)))
    (CDR C)))))))

(TH (LAMBDA (A1 A2 C1 C2) (COND ((NULL A2) (AND (NOT (NULL C2))
    (THR (CAR C2) A1 A2 C1 (CDR C2)))) (T (THL (CAR A2) A1 (CDR A2)
    C1 C2)))))

(THL (LAMBDA (U A1 A2 C1 C2) (COND
    ((EQ (CAR U) (QUOTE NOT)) (TH1R (CADR U) A1 A2 C1 C2))
    ((EQ (CAR U) (QUOTE AND)) (TH2L (CDR U) A1 A2 C1 C2))
    ((EQ (CAR U) (QUOTE OR)) (AND (TH1L (CADR U) A1 A2 C1 C2)
    (TH1L (CADDR U) A1 A2 C1 C2) ))
    ((EQ (CAR U) (QUOTE IMPLIES)) (AND (TH1L (CADDR U) A1 A2 C1
    C2) (TH1R (CADR U) A1 A2 C1 C2) ))
    ((EQ (CAR U) (QUOTE EQUIV)) (AND (TH2L (CDR U) A1 A2 C1 C2)
    (TH2R (CDR U) A1 A2 C1 C2) ))
    (T (ERROR (LIST (QUOTE THL) U A1 A2 C1 C2)))
    )))

(THR (LAMBDA (U A1 A2 C1 C2) (COND
    ((EQ (CAR U) (QUOTE NOT)) (TH1L (CADR U) A1 A2 C1 C2))
    ((EQ (CAR U) (QUOTE AND)) (AND (TH1R (CADR U) A1 A2 C1 C2)
    (TH1R (CADDR U) A1 A2 C1 C2) ))
    ((EQ (CAR U) (QUOTE OR)) (TH2R (CDR U) A1 A2 C1 C2))
    ((EQ (CAR U) (QUOTE IMPLIES)) (TH11 (CADR U) (CADDR U)
```

```
            A1 A2 C1 C2))
         ((EQ (CAR U) (QUOTE EQUIV)) (AND (TH11 (CADR U) (CADDR U)
            A1 A2 C1 C2) (TH11 (CADDR U) (CADR U) A1 A2 C1 C2) ))
         (T (ERROR (LIST (QUOTE THR) U A1 A2 C1 C2)))
         )))

(TH1L (LAMBDA (V A1 A2 C1 C2) (COND
      ((ATOM V) (OR (MEMBER V C1)
      (TH (CONS V A1) A2 C1 C2) ))
      (T (OR (MEMBER V C2) (TH A1 (CONS V A2) C1 C2) ))
      )))

(TH1R (LAMBDA (V A1 A2 C1 C2) (COND
      ((ATOM V) (OR (MEMBER V A1)
      (TH A1 A2 (CONS V C1) C2) ))
      (T (OR (MEMBER V A2) (TH A1 A2 C1 (CONS V C2))))
      )))



(TH2L (LAMBDA (V A1 A2 C1 C2) (COND
      ((ATOM (CAR V)) (OR (MEMBER (CAR V) C1)
      (TH1L (CADR V) (CONS (CAR V) A1) A2 C1 C2)))
      (T (OR (MEMBER (CAR V) C2) (TH1L (CADR V) A1 (CONS (CAR V)
      A2) C1 C2)))
      )))

(TH2R (LAMBDA (V A1 A2 C1 C2) (COND
      ((ATOM (CAR V)) (OR (MEMBER (CAR V) A1)
      (TH1R (CADR V) A1 A2 (CONS (CAR V) C1) C2)))
      (T (OR (MEMBER (CAR V) A2) (TH1R (CADR V) A1 A2 C1
      (CONS (CAR V) C2))))
      )))

(TH11 (LAMBDA (V1 V2 A1 A2 C1 C2) (COND
      ((ATOM V1) (OR (MEMBER V1 C1) (TH1R V2 (CONS V1 A1) A2 C1
      C2)))
      (T (OR (MEMBER V1 C2) (TH1R V2 A1 (CONS V1 A2) C1 C2)))
      )))
   ))
```

TRACE ((THEOREM TH1 TH2 TH THL THR TH1L TH1R TH2L TH2R TH11))

THEOREM
((ARROW (P) ((OR P Q))))

UNTRACE ((THEOREM TH1 TH2 THR THL TH1L TH1R TH2L TH2R TH11))

THEOREM
((ARROW ((OR A (NOT B))) ((IMPLIES (AND P Q) (EQUIV P Q)))))

STOP)))   )))   )))   )))
        FIN   END OF LISP RUN   M948-1207   LEVIN

This run produced the following output:

* M948-1207 LEVIN, LISP, TEST, 2, 3, 250, 0
        TEST   WANG ALGORITHM FOR THE PROPOSITIONAL CALCULUS
THE TIME (8/ 8 1506.1) HAS COME, THE WALRUS SAID, TO TALK OF MANY THINGS
... — LEWIS CARROLL —

 FUNCTION   EVALQUOTE   HAS BEEN ENTERED, ARGUMENTS..
DEFINE
[The complete list of definitions read in is omitted to save space.]

END OF EVALQUOTE, VALUE IS..
(THEOREM TH1 TH2 TH THL THR TH1L TH1R TH2L TH2R TH11)

 FUNCTION   EVALQUOTE   HAS BEEN ENTERED, ARGUMENTS..
TRACE
((THEOREM TH1 TH2 TH THL THR TH1L TH1R TH2L TH2R TH11))

END OF EVALQUOTE, VALUE IS..
NIL

 FUNCTION   EVALQUOTE   HAS BEEN ENTERED, ARGUMENTS..
THEOREM
((ARROW (P) ((OR P Q))))

ARGUMENTS OF TH1
NIL
NIL
(P)
((OR P Q))

ARGUMENTS OF TH1
(P)
NIL
NIL
((OR P Q))

ARGUMENTS OF TH2
(P)
NIL
NIL
NIL
((OR P Q))

ARGUMENTS OF TH2
(P)
NIL
NIL
((OR P Q))
NIL

ARGUMENTS OF TH
(P)
NIL
NIL
((OR P Q))

ARGUMENTS OF THR
(OR P Q)
(P)
NIL
NIL
NIL

ARGUMENTS OF TH2R
(P Q)

(P)
NIL
NIL
NIL

VALUE OF TH2R
T

VALUE OF THR
T

VALUE OF TH
T

VALUE OF TH2
T

VALUE OF TH2
T

VALUE OF TH1
T

VALUE OF TH1
T

END OF EVALQUOTE, VALUE IS..
T

   FUNCTION   EVALQUOTE   HAS BEEN ENTERED, ARGUMENTS..
UNTRACE
((THEOREM TH1 TH2 THR THL TH1L TH1R TH2L TH2R TH11))

END OF EVALQUOTE, VALUE IS ..
NIL

   FUNCTION   EVALQUOTE   HAS BEEN ENTERED, ARGUMENTS..
THEOREM
((ARROW ((OR A (NOT B))) ((IMPLIES (AND P Q) (EQUIV P Q)))))

ARGUMENTS OF TH
NIL
((OR A (NOT B)))
NIL
((IMPLIES (AND P Q) (EQUIV P Q)))

ARGUMENTS OF TH
(A)
NIL
NIL
((IMPLIES (AND P Q) (EQUIV P Q)))

ARGUMENTS OF TH
(A)
((AND P Q))
NIL
((EQUIV P Q))

ARGUMENTS OF TH
(Q P A)
NIL
NIL
((EQUIV P Q))

VALUE OF TH
T

VALUE OF TH
T

VALUE OF TH
T

ARGUMENTS OF TH
NIL
((NOT B))
NIL
((IMPLIES (AND P Q) (EQUIV P Q)))

ARGUMENTS OF TH
NIL

NIL
(B)
((IMPLIES (AND P Q) (EQUIV P Q))

ARGUMENTS OF TH
NIL
((AND P Q))
(B)
((EQUIV P Q))

ARGUMENTS OF TH
(Q P)
NIL
(B)
((EQUIV P Q))

VALUE OF TH
T

VALUE OF TH
T

VALUE OF TH
T

VALUE OF TH
T

VALUE OF TH
T

END OF EVALQUOTE, VALUE IS..
T

THE TIME (8/ 8 1506. 3) HAS COME, THE WALRUS SAID, TO TALK OF MANY THINGS
... – LEWIS CARROLL –

END OF EVALQUOTE OPERATOR

        FIN   END OF LISP RUN   M948-1207   LEVIN

END OF LISP JOB

APPENDIX A

FUNCTIONS AND CONSTANTS IN THE LISP SYSTEM

This appendix contains all functions available in the LISP System as of August 1962.

Each entry contains the name of the object, the property under which it is available (e.g., EXPR, FEXPR, SUBR, FSUBR, or APVAL), whether it is a pseudo-function, functional (function having functions as arguments), or predicate, and in some cases a definition of the function as an M-expression. In the case of APVAL's, the value is given.

The LISP Library is a file of BCD cards distributed with the LISP System. It is not intended to be used as input to the computer without being edited first. Have the Library file punched out, and then list the cards. Each Library function is preceded by a title card that must be removed. Some Library entries are in the form of a DEFINE, while some are in the form of an assembly in LAP. Note that some of them have auxiliary functions that must be included.

Elementary Functions

car[x]   :   SUBR
cdr[x]   :   SUBR

The elementary functions car and cdr always have some sort of value rather than giving an error diagnostic. A chain of cdr's applied to an atomic symbol will allow one to search its property list. Indiscriminate use of these functions past the atomic level will result in non-list structure and may appear as lengthy or even infinite garbage expressions if printed.

```
CAR      SXA      CARX,4
         PDX      0,4
         CLA      0,4
         PAX      0,4
         PXD      0,4
CARX     AXT      **,4
         TRA      1,4

CDR      SXA      CDRX,4
         PDX      0,4
         CLA      0,4
         PDX      0,4
         PXD      0,4
CDRX     AXT      **,4
         TRA      1,4
```

cons[x;y]   :   SUBR

cons obtains a new word from the free storage list and places its two arguments in the address and decrement of this word, respectively. It does not check to see if the arguments are valid list structure. The value of cons is a pointer to the word that

56

was just created. If the free storage list has been exhausted, <u>cons</u> calls the garbage collector to make a new free storage list and then performs the <u>cons</u> operation.

<u>atom</u>[x]   :   SUBR   predicate

The first word on the property list of an atomic symbol contains −1 or 77777_8 in the address. The following subroutine depends upon this, and on the fact that NIL is located at 0 and *T* is located at −1 and has 1 as its complement pointer.

```
ATOM      SXA    ATOMX, 4
          PDX    0, 4
          CLA    0, 4         GET CAR OF ARGUMENT
          PAX    0, 4
          TXL    *+3, 4, -2   TRANSFER IF NOT ATOMIC
          CLA    TRUE         IF IT IS ATOMIC
          TRA    *+2
          PXA    0, 0         NIL IF NOT ATOMIC
ATOMX     AXT    **, 4
          TRA    1, 4
TRUE      OCT    1000000
```

<u>eq</u>[x;y]   :   SUBR   predicate

<u>eq</u> is true if its two arguments are identical list structure.

```
EQ        STQ    X
          SUB    X
          TZE    *+3          TRANSFER IF EQUAL
          PXA    0, 0         OTHERWISE VALUE IS NIL
          TRA    1, 4
          CLA    TRUE         VALUE IS *T*
          TRA    1, 4
TRUE      OCT    1000000
X         PZE
```

<u>equal</u>[x;y]   :   SUBR   predicate

<u>equal</u> is true if its arguments are the same S-expression, although they do not have to be identical list structure in the computer. It uses <u>eq</u> on the atomic level and is recursive. Floating point numbers in S-expressions are compared for numerical equality with a floating point tolerance of 3×10^{-6}. Fixed point numbers are compared for numerical equality.

<u>list</u>[x_1; ... ;x_n]   :   FSUBR

The value of <u>list</u> is a list of its arguments.

<u>null</u>[x]   :   SUBR   predicate

The value of <u>null</u> is true if its argument is NIL which is located at 0 in the computer.

```
NULL      TZE    *+3
          PXA    0, 0
          TRA    1, 4
          CLA    TRUE
          TRA    1, 4
TRUE      OCT    1000000
```

rplaca[x;y]　　　　　:　　SUBR　　　pseudo-function

rplacd[x;y]　　　　　:　　SUBR　　　pseudo-function

These list operators change list structure and can damage the system memory if not used properly. See page 41 for a description of usage.

Logical Connectives

$\underline{and}[x_1;x_2\ldots;x_n]$　　:　　FSUBR　　predicate

The arguments of $\underline{and}$ are evaluated in sequence, from left to right, until one is found that is false, or until the end of the list is reached. The value of $\underline{and}$ is false or true respectively.

$\underline{or}[x_1;x_2\ldots;x_n]$　　:　　FSUBR　　predicate

The arguments of $\underline{or}$ are evaluated in sequence from left to right, until one is found that is true, or until the end of the list is reached. The value of $\underline{or}$ is true or false respectively.

$\underline{not}[x]$　　　　　　:　　SUBR　　　predicate

The value of $\underline{not}$ is true if its argument is false, and false otherwise.

Interpreter and Prog Feature

These are described elsewhere in the manual:
APPLY, EVAL, EVLIS, QUOTE, LABEL, FUNCTION, PROG, GO, RETURN, SET, SETQ.

Defining Functions and Functions Useful for Property Lists

$\underline{define}[x]$　　　　　:　　EXPR　　　pseudo-function

The argument of $\underline{define}$, x, is a list of pairs
$$((u_1 \ v_1) \ (u_2 \ v_2) \ \ldots \ (u_n \ v_n))$$
where each u is a name and each v is a λ-expression for a function. For each pair, $\underline{define}$ puts an EXPR on the property list for u pointing to v. The function of $\underline{define}$ puts things on at the front of the property list. The value of define is the list of u's.

define[x] = deflist[x;EXPR]

$\underline{deflist}[x;ind]$　　　　:　　EXPR　　　pseudo-function

The function $\underline{deflist}$ is a more general defining function. Its first argument is a list of pairs as for $\underline{define}$. Its second argument is the indicator that is to be used. After $\underline{deflist}$ has been executed with $(u_i \ v_i)$ among its first argument, the property list of u_i will begin:

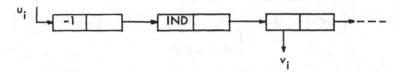

If <u>deflist</u> or <u>define</u> is used twice on the same object with the same indicator, the old value will be replaced by the new one.

<u>attrib</u>[x;e]   :   SUBR   pseudo-function

The function <u>attrib</u> concatenates its two arguments by changing the last element of its first argument to point to the second argument. Thus it is commonly used to tack something onto the end of a property list. The value of <u>attrib</u> is the second argument. For example

attrib[FF; (EXPR (LAMBDA (X) (COND ((ATOM X) X) (T (FF (CAR X))))))]

would put EXPR followed by the LAMBDA expression for FF onto the end of the property list for FF.

<u>prop</u>[x;y;u]   :   SUBR   functional

The function <u>prop</u> searches the list x for an item that is <u>eq</u> to y. If such an element is found, the value of <u>prop</u> is the rest of the list beginning immediately after the element. Otherwise the value is $\underline{u}$[ ], where $\underline{u}$ is a function of no arguments.

$$\text{prop}[x;y;u] = [\text{null}[x] \to u[\ ]; \text{eq}[\text{car}[x];y] \to \text{cdr}[x];$$
$$T \to \text{prop}[\text{cdr}[x];y;u]]$$

<u>get</u>[x;y]   :   SUBR

<u>get</u> is somewhat like <u>prop</u>; however its value is <u>car</u> of the rest of the list if the indicator is found, and NIL otherwise.

$$\text{get}[x;y] = [\text{null}[x] \to \text{NIL}; \text{eq}[\text{car}[x];y] \to \text{cadr}[x];$$
$$T \to \text{get}[\text{cdr}[x];y]]$$

<u>cset</u>[ob;val]   :   EXPR   pseudo-function

This pseudo-function is used to create a constant by putting the indicator APVAL and a value on the property list of an atomic symbol. The first argument should be an atomic symbol; the second argument is the value is cons[val;NIL].

<u>csetq</u>[ob;val]   :   FEXPR   pseudo-function

<u>csetq</u> is like <u>cset</u> except that it quotes its first argument instead of evaluating it.

<u>remprop</u>[x;ind]   :   SUBR   pseudo-function

The pseudo-function <u>remprop</u> searches the list, x, looking for all occurrences of the indicator ind. When such an indicator is found, its name and the succeeding property are removed from the list. The two "ends" of the list are tied together as indicated by the dashed line below.

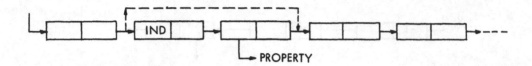

PROPERTY

The value of <u>remprop</u> is NIL.

When an indicator appears on a property list without a property following it, then it is called a flag. An example of a flag is the indicator TRACE which informs the interpreter that the function on whose property list it appears is to be traced. There are two pseudo-functions for creating and removing flags respectively.

<u>flag</u>[ℓ;ind]   :   **EXPR**   pseudo-function

The pseudo-function <u>flag</u> puts the flag ind on the property list of every atomic symbol in the list ℓ. Note that ℓ cannot be an atomic symbol, and must be a list of atomic symbols. The flag is always placed immediately following the first word of the property list, and the rest of the property list then follows. The value of <u>flag</u> is NIL. No property list ever receives a duplicated flag.

<u>remflag</u>[ℓ;ind]   :   **EXPR**   pseudo-function

<u>remflag</u> removes all occurrences of the indicator ind from the property list of each atomic symbol in the list ℓ. It does this by patching around the indicator with a <u>rplacd</u> in a manner similar to the way <u>remprop</u> works.

Table Building and Table Reference Functions

<u>pair</u>[x;y]   :   **SUBR**

The function <u>pair</u> has as value the list of pairs of corresponding elements of the lists x and y. The arguments x and y must be lists of the same number of elements. They should <u>not</u> be atomic symbols. The value is a dotted pair list, i.e. $((a_1 \cdot \beta_1)(a_2 \cdot \beta_2)\dots$

$$\text{pair}[x;y] = [\text{prog}[u;v;m]$$
$$u := x;$$
$$v := y;$$

A $[\text{null}[u] \rightarrow [\text{null}[v] \rightarrow \text{return}[m];T \rightarrow \text{error}[F2]]];$
$[\text{null}[v] \rightarrow \text{error}[F3]];$
$m := \text{cons}[\text{cons}[\text{car}[u];\text{car}[v]];m];$
$u := \text{cdr}[u];$
$v := \text{cdr}[v];$
$\text{go}[A]]$

<u>sassoc</u>[x;y;u]   :   **SUBR**   functional

The function <u>sassoc</u> searches y, which is a list of dotted pairs, for a pair whose first element that is x. If such a pair is found, the value of <u>sassoc</u> is this pair. Otherwise the function u of no arguments is taken as the value of <u>sassoc</u>.

$$sassoc[x;y;u] = [null[y] \rightarrow u[];eq[caar[y];x] \rightarrow car[y];$$
$$T \rightarrow sassoc[x;cdr[y];u]]$$

<u>subst</u>[x;y;z]   :   SUBR

The function <u>subst</u> has as value the result of substituting x for all occurrences of the S-expression y in the S-expression z.

$$subst[x;y;z] = [equal[y;z] \rightarrow x;$$
$$atom[z] \rightarrow z;$$
$$T \rightarrow cons[subst[x;y;car[z]];subst[x;y;cdr[z]]]]$$

<u>sublis</u>[x;y]   :   SUBR

Here x is a list of pairs,
$$((u_1 \cdot v_1)\ (u_2 \cdot v_2) \ldots (u_n \cdot v_n))$$

The value of <u>sublis</u>[x;y] is the result of substituting each v for the corresponding u in y.

Note that the following M-expression is different from that given in Section I, though the result is the same.

$$sublis[x;y] = [null[x] \rightarrow y;$$
$$null[y] \rightarrow y;$$
$$T \rightarrow search[x;$$
$$\lambda[[j];equal[y;caar[j]]];$$
$$\lambda[[j];cdar[j]];$$
$$\lambda[[j];[atom[y] \rightarrow y;$$
$$T \rightarrow cons[sublis[x;car[y]];sublis[x;cdr[y]]]]]]]]$$

List Handling Functions

append[x;y]   :   SUBR

The function <u>append</u> combines its two arguments into one new list. The value of append is the resultant list. For example,

    append[(A B) (C)] = (A B C)

    append[((A)) (C D)] = ((A) C D)

    append[x;y] = [null[x] \rightarrow y;T \rightarrow cons[car[x];append[cdr[x];y]]]

Note that <u>append</u> copies the top level of the first list; <u>append</u> is like <u>nconc</u> except that <u>nconc</u> does not copy its first argument.

<u>conc</u>[$x_1;x_2;\ldots;x_n$]   :   FEXPR   pseudo-function

<u>conc</u> concatenates its arguments by stringing them all together on the top level. For example,

    conc[(A (B $\cdot$ C) D); (F); (G H)] = (A (B $\cdot$ C) D F G H).

<u>conc</u> concatenates its arguments without copying them. Thus it changes existing list structure and is a pseudo-function. The value of <u>conc</u> is the resulting concatenated list.

61

nconc[x;y]　　　　：　　　SUBR　　　　pseudo-function

The function <u>nconc</u> concatenates its arguments without copying the first one. The operation is identical to that of <u>attrib</u> except that the value is the entire result, (i.e. the modified first argument, x).

The program for nconc[x;y] has the program variable m and is as follows:

nconc[x;y] = prog[[m];
　　　　[null[x] → return[y]];
　　　　m:=x;
A　　　[null[cdr[m]] → go[B]];
　　　　m:=cdr[m];
　　　　go[A];
B　　　rplacd[m;y];
　　　　return[x]]

copy[x]　　　　：　　　SUBR

This function makes a copy of the list x. The value of <u>copy</u> is the location of the copied list.

copy[x] = [null[x] → NIL;atom[x] → x;T → cons[copy[car[x]];
　　　　copy[cdr[x]]]]

reverse[ℓ]　　　　：　　　SUBR

This is a function to reverse the top level of a list. Thus
reverse[(A B (C · D))] = ((C · D) B A))
reverse[ℓ] = prog[[v];
　　　　u:=ℓ;
A　　　[null[u] → return[v]];
　　　　v:=cons[car[u];v];
　　　　u:=cdr[u];
　　　　go[A]]

member[x;ℓ]　　　　：　　　SUBR　　　　predicate

If the S-expression x is a member of the list ℓ, then the value of <u>member</u> is *T*. Otherwise, the value is NIL.

member[x;ℓ] = [null[ℓ] → F;equal[x;car[ℓ]] → T;
　　　　T → member[x;cdr[ℓ]]]

length[x]　　　　：　　　SUBR

The value of <u>length</u> is the number of items in the list x. The list ( ) or NIL has <u>length</u> 0.

efface[x;ℓ]   :   SUBR   pseudo-function

The function efface deletes the first appearance of the item x from the list ℓ.

efface[x;ℓ] = [null[ℓ] → NIL;
                equal[x;car[ℓ]] → cdr[ℓ];
                T → rplacd[ℓ;efface[x;cdr[ℓ]]]]

These four functionals apply a function, f, to x, then to cdr[x], then to cddr[x], etc.

Functionals or Functions with Functions as Arguments

maplist[x;f]   :   SUBR   functional

The function maplist is a mapping of the list x onto a new list f[x].
maplist[x;f] = [null[x] → NIL;T → cons[f[x];maplist[cdr[x];f]]]

mapcon[x;f]   :   SUBR   pseudo-functional

The function mapcon is like the function maplist except that the resultant list is a concatenated one instead of having been created by cons-ing.
mapcon[x;f] = [null[x] → NIL;T → nconc[f[x];mapcon[cdr[x];f]]]

map[x;f]   :   SUBR   functional

The function map is like the function maplist except that the value of map is NIL, and map does not do a cons of the evaluated functions. map is used only when the action of doing f[x] is important.

The program for map[x;f] has the program variable m and is the following:
map[x;f] = prog[[m];
        m:= x;
LOOP [null[m] → return[NIL]];
        f[m];
        m:= cdr[m];
        go[LOOP]]

search[x;p;f;u]   :   SUBR   functional

The function search looks through a list x for an element that has the property p, and if such an element is found the function f of that element is the value of search. If there is no such element, the function u of one argument x is taken as the value of search (in this case x is, of course, NIL).

search[x;p;f;u] = [null[x] → u[x];p[x] → f[x];T → search[cdr[x];p;f;u]]

Arithmetic Functions

These are discussed at length in Section IV.

function	type	number of args	value
plus	FSUBR	indef.	$x_1+x_2+\ldots+x_n$
minus	SUBR	1	$-x$

63

difference	SUBR		2	$x-y$
times	FSUBR		indef.	$x_1 \cdot x_2 \cdot \ldots \cdot x_n$
divide	SUBR		2	$list[x/y;remainder]$
quotient	SUBR		2	x/y
remainder	SUBR		2	remainder of x/y
add1	SUBR		1	$x+1$
sub1	SUBR		1	$x-1$
max	FSUBR		indef.	largest of x_i
min	FSUBR		indef.	smallest of x_i
recip	SUBR		1	$[fixp[x] \rightarrow 0; T \rightarrow quotient[1;x]]$
expt	SUBR		2	x^y
lessp	SUBR	predicate	2	$x < y$
greaterp	SUBR	predicate	2	$x > y$
zerop	SUBR	predicate	1	$|x| \leq 3 \times 10^{-6}$
onep	SUBR	predicate	1	$|x - 1| \leq 3 \times 10^{-6}$
minusp	SUBR	predicate	1	x is negative
numberp	SUBR	predicate	1	x is a number
fixp	SUBR	predicate	1	x is a fixed point number
floatp	SUBR	predicate	1	x is a floating point no.
logor	FSUBR		indef.	$x_1 \vee x_2 \vee \ldots \vee x_n$ ORA
logand	FSUBR		indef.	$x_1 \wedge x_2 \wedge \ldots \wedge x_n$ ANA
logxor	FSUBR		indef.	$x_1 \veebar x_2 \veebar \ldots \veebar x_n$ ERA
leftshift	SUBR		2	$x \cdot 2^y$
array	SUBR		1	declares arrays

The Compiler and Assembler

compile[x]   :   SUBR   pseudo-function

The list x contains the names of previously defined functions. They are compiled.

special[x]   :   SUBR   pseudo-function

The list x contains the names of variables that are to be declared SPECIAL.

unspecial[x]   :   SUBR   pseudo-function

The list x contains the names of variables that are no longer to be considered SPECIAL by the compiler.

common[x]   :   SUBR   pseudo-function

The list x contains the names of variables that are to be declared COMMON.

uncommon[x]   :   SUBR   pseudo-function

The list x contains the names of variables that are no longer to be considered COMMON by the compiler.

lap[list;table] : SUBR pseudo-function

The assembler LAP is discussed in appendix C.

opdefine[x] : EXPR pseudo-function

opdefine defines new symbols for the assembler LAP. The argument is a list of dotted pairs, each pair consisting of symbol and value.

readlap[ ] : EXPR pseudo-function

readlap reads assembly language input and causes it to be assembled using LAP. The input follows the STOP card of the packet containing the readlap. Each function to be read in consists of a list of the two arguments of lap. These are read in successively until a card containing NIL is encountered. readlap uses remob to remove unwanted atomic symbols occurring in the listing. For this reason, it should only be used to read cards that have been produced by punchlap.

Input and Output

read[ ] : SUBR pseudo-function

The execution of read causes one list to be read from SYSPIT, or from the card reader. The list that is read is the value of read.

print[x] : SUBR pseudo-function

The execution of print causes the S-expression x to be printed on SYSPOT and/or the on-line printer. The value of print is its argument.

punch[x] : SUBR pseudo-function

The execution of punch causes S-expression x to be punched in BCD card images on SYSPPT. The value of punch is its argument.

print[x] : SUBR pseudo-function

print prints an atomic symbol without terminating the print line. The argument of print must be an atomic symbol.

terpri[ ] : SUBR pseudo-function

terpri terminates the print line.

The character reading, sorting and printing functions are discussed in appendix F.

startread	pack	opchar	error1	numob
advance	unpack	dash		mknam
endread		digit		
clearbuff		liter		

Functions for System Control, Debugging, and Error Processing

trace[x]   :   EXPR   pseudo-function

The argument of trace is a list of functions. After trace has been executed, the arguments and values of these functions are printed each time the function is entered recursively. This is illustrated in the printed output of the Wang Algorithm example. The value of trace is NIL. Special forms cannot be traced.

untrace[x]   :   EXPR   pseudo-function

This removes the tracing from all functions in the list x. The value of untrace is NIL.

The following pseudo-functions are described in the section on running the LISP system:

count, uncount, speak, error, errorset.

Miscellaneous Functions

prog2 [x;y]   :   SUBR

The value of prog2 is its second argument. It is used mainly to perform two pseudo-functions.

prog2 [x;y] = y

cp1 [x]   :   SUBR

cp1 copies its argument which must be a list of a very special type.

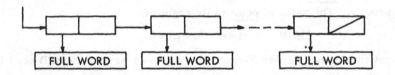

The copied list is the value of cp1.

gensym[ ]   :   SUBR

The function gensym has no arguments. Its value is a new, distinct, and freshly-created atomic symbol with a print name of the form G00001, G00002, ..., G99999.

This function is useful for creating atomic symbols when one is needed; each one is guaranteed unique. gensym names are not permanent and will not be recognized if read back in.

select[q;(q_1 e_1);(q_2 e_2); ...;(q_n e_n);e]   :   FEXPR

The q_i's in select are evaluated in sequence from left to right until one is found that

$$q_i = q,$$

and the value of select is the value of the corresponding e_i. If no such q_i is found the value of select is that of e.

tempus-fugit[ ]   :   SUBR   pseudo-function

Executing this will cause a time statement to appear in the output. The value is NIL. (tempus-fugit is for MIT users only.)

load[ ]   :   SUBR   pseudo-function

Program control is given to the LISP loader which expects octal correction cards, 704 row binary cards, and a transfer card.

plb [ ]   :   SUBR   pseudo-function

This is equivalent to pushing "LOAD CARDS" on the console in the middle of a LISP program.

reclaim[ ]   :   SUBR   pseudo-function

Executing this will cause a garbage collection to occur. The value is NIL.

pause[ ]   :   SUBR   pseudo-function

Executing this will cause a program halt. Pushing START will cause the program to continue, returning the value NIL.

excise[x]   :   SUBR   pseudo-function

If x is NIL, then the compiler will be overwritten with free storage. If x is *T*, then both the compiler and LAP will be overwritten by free storage. excise may be executed more than once. The effect of excise[*T*] is somewhat unreliable. It is recommended that before executing this pair, remprop [*;SYM] be executed.

dump[low;high;mode;title]   :   SUBR   pseudo-function

dump causes memory to be dumped in octal. The dump is from location low to location high. If the mode is 0, then the dump is straight. If the mode is 1, the words containing zero in the prefix and tag will be dumped as complement decrements and addresses. This is convenient for examining list structure.

intern[x]   :   SUBR   pseudo-function

The argument of intern must be a PNAME type of structure, that is, a list of full words forming a print name. If this print name belongs to an already existing atomic symbol, this is found, otherwise a new one is created. The value of intern in either case is an atomic symbol having the specified print name.

remob[x]   :   SUBR

This removes the atom x from the object list. It causes the symbol and all its properties to be lost unless the symbol is referred to by active list structure. When an atomic symbol has been removed, subsequent reading of its name from input will create a different atomic symbol.

The LISP Library

The LISP Library is distributed as the second file on the LISP setup tape. To use any part of it, punch out the entire library and remove the part you wish to use. Be sure to strip off comment cards, unnecessary DEFINE cards, and unnecessary cards that close a define with)).

Some entries in the library have several parts or define more than one function.

traceset[x]   :   EXPR   pseudo-function

traceset is a debugging aid. The argument x should be a list of functions names. Each of these functions must be an EXPR which has a PROG on the top level. traceset modifies the definition of the function so that every SETQ on the first level inside the PROG is traced.

For example, suppose a PROG has the statement (SETQ A X). At run time, if this statment is executed while x has the value (U V), then in addition to setting the variable a, the function will print out:

(A =)

(U V)

untraceset[x] is part of the traceset package. Its argument is a list of functions whose definitions are to be restored to their original condition.

punchlap[ ]   :   EXPR   pseudo-function

punchlap allows one to compile functions and have the results punched out in assembly language LAP. The punched output is in a format suitable for readlap. The functions to be compiled into LAP are placed at the end of the packet following the STOP card. Each one is read individually and the result is punched out. No assembling into memory takes place. The process stops when a card containing the word NIL is encountered after the last function.

Each function must consist of a list of the form (name exp) which is the exact form for insertion into a define.

Part of punchlap is a dummy definition of lap. This prevents lap from being used within the memory of this packet. The printout from punchlap is not a copy of the cards produced; only the internal functions have their LAP printed. The PNAMEs of atoms in the EXPRs and FEXPRs of punchlapped functions must not contain class C characters.

printprop[x]   :   EXPR   pseudo-function

If x is an atomic symbol, all of its properties will be printed in the output. Nothing is changed by printprop.

punchdef[x]   :   EXPR   pseudo-function

If x is a list of atomic symbols, each one having an EXPR or FEXPR will have its definition punched out. Nothing is changed.

APVAL's

The following is a list of all atoms with APVAL's on their property lists in the basic system and their values.

APVAL	value
BLANK	(BCD blank)
CHARCOUNT	(character count during reading of characters)
COMMA	,
CURCHAR	(current character during reading of characters)
DOLLAR	$
EOF	EOF
EOR	EOR
EQSIGN	=
F	NIL
LPAR	(
NIL	NIL
OBLIST[1]	(bucket sorted object list)
PERIOD	.
PLUSS	+
RPAR	)
SLASH	/
STAR	*
T	*T*
T	*T*

---

1. The entire set of objects (atomic symbols) existing in the system can be printed out by performing

        EVAL (OBLIST NIL).

APPENDIX B

THE LISP INTERPRETER

This appendix is written in mixed M-expressions and English. Its purpose is to describe as closely as possible the actual working of the interpreter and PROG feature. The functions evalquote, apply, eval, evlis, evcon, and the PROG feature are defined by using a language that follows the M-expression notation as closely as possible and contains some insertions in English.

$$evalquote[fn;args]=[get\,[fn;FEXPR]\,\vee get\,[fn;FSUBR]\rightarrow$$
$$eval[cons[\,fn;args\,];NIL]$$
$$T\rightarrow apply[fn;args;NIL]]$$

This definition shows that evalquote is capable of handling special forms as a sort of exception. Apply cannot handle special forms and will give error A2 if given one as its first argument.

The following definition of apply is an enlargement of the one given in Section I. It shows how functional arguments bound by FUNARG are processed, and describes the way in which machine language subroutines are called.

In this description, spread can be regarded as a pseudo-function of one argument. This argument is a list. spread puts the individual items of this list into the AC, MQ, $ARG3, ... the standard cells for transmitting arguments to functions.

These M-expressions should not be taken too literally. In many cases, the actual program is a store and transfer where a recursion is suggested by these definitions.

$$apply[fn;args;a]=[$$
$$null[fn]\rightarrow NIL;$$
$$atom[fn]\rightarrow[get[fn;EXPR]\rightarrow apply[expr^1\!;args;a];$$
$$get[fn;SUBR]\rightarrow \left\{ \begin{array}{l} spread[args]; \\ \$ALIST:=a; \\ TSX\ subr^1,4 \end{array} \right\} ;$$
$$T\rightarrow apply[cdr[sassoc[fn;a;\lambda[[];error[A2]]]];args;a];$$
$$eq[car[fn];LABEL]\rightarrow apply[caddr[fn];args;cons[cons[cadr[fn];caddr[fn]];a]];$$
$$eq[car[fn];FUNARG]\rightarrow apply[cadr[fn];args;caddr[fn]];$$
$$eq[car[fn];LAMBDA]\rightarrow eval[caddr[fn];nconc[pair[cadr[fn];args];a]];$$
$$T\rightarrow apply[eval[fn;a];args;a]]$$

---

1. The value of get is set aside. This is the meaning of the apparent free or undefined variable.

$$\underline{\text{eval}}[\text{form};a]=[$$
$$\text{null}[\text{form}]\rightarrow\text{NIL};$$
$$\text{numberp}[\text{form}]\rightarrow\text{form};$$
$$\text{atom}[\text{form}]\rightarrow[\text{get}[\text{form};\text{APVAL}]\rightarrow\text{car}[\text{apval}^1];$$
$$\text{T}\rightarrow\text{cdr}[\text{sassoc}[\text{form};a;\lambda[[\ ];\text{error}[\text{A8}]]]]];$$
$$\text{eq}[\text{car}[\text{form}];\text{QUOTE}]\rightarrow\text{cadr}[\text{form}];^2$$
$$\text{eq}[\text{car}[\text{form}];\text{FUNCTION}]\rightarrow\text{list}[\text{FUNARG};\text{cadr}[\text{form}];a];^2$$
$$\text{eq}[\text{car}[\text{form}];\text{COND}]\rightarrow\text{evcon}[\text{cdr}[\text{form}];a];$$
$$\text{eq}[\text{car}[\text{form}];\text{PROG}]\rightarrow\text{prog}[\text{cdr}[\text{form}];a];^2$$
$$\text{atom}[\text{car}[\text{form}]]\rightarrow[\text{get}[\text{car}[\text{form}];\text{EXPR}]\rightarrow\text{apply}[\text{expr};^1\text{evlis}[\text{cdr}[\text{form}];a];a];$$
$$\text{get}[\text{car}[\text{form}];\text{FEXPR}]\rightarrow\text{apply}[\text{fexpr};^1\text{list}[\text{cdr}[\text{form}];a];a];$$

$$\text{get}[\text{car}[\text{form}];\text{SUBR}]\rightarrow\left\{\begin{array}{l}\text{spread}[\text{evlis}[\text{cdr}[\text{form}];a]];\\ \text{\$ALIST:}=a;\\ \text{TSX subr},^1 4\end{array}\right\};$$

$$\text{get}[\text{car}[\text{form}];\text{FSUBR}]\rightarrow\left\{\begin{array}{l}\text{AC:}=\text{cdr}[\text{form}];\\ \text{MQ:}=\text{\$ALIST:}=a;\\ \text{TSX fsubr},^1 4\end{array}\right\};$$

$$\text{T}\rightarrow\text{eval}[\text{cons}[\text{cdr}[\text{sassoc}[\text{car}[\text{form}];a;\lambda[[];\text{error}[\text{A9}]]]];$$
$$\text{cdr}[\text{form}]];a]];$$
$$\text{T}\rightarrow\text{apply}[\text{car}[\text{form}];\text{evlis}[\text{cdr}[\text{form}];a];a]]$$
$$\underline{\text{evcon}}[c;a]=[\text{null}[c]\rightarrow\text{error}[\text{A3}];$$
$$\text{eval}[\text{caar}[c];a]\rightarrow\text{eval}[\text{cadar}[a];a];$$
$$\text{T}\rightarrow\text{evcon}[\text{cdr}[c];a]]$$

$$\underline{\text{evlis}}[m;a]=\text{maplist}[m;\lambda[[j];\text{eval}[\text{car}[j];a]]]$$

The PROG Feature

The PROG feature is an FSUBR coded into the system. It can best be explained in English, although it is possible to define it by using M-expressions.

1. As soon as the PROG feature is entered, the list of program variables is used to make a new list in which each one is paired with NIL. This is then appended to the current a-list. Thus each program variable is set to NIL at the entrance to the program.

2. The remainder of the program is searched for atomic symbols that are understood to be location symbols. A go-list is formed in which each location symbol is paired with a pointer into the remainder of the program.

3. When a set or a setq is encountered, the name of the variable is located on the a-list. The value of the variable (or cdr of the pair) is actually replaced with the new value.

---

1. The value of get is set aside. This is the meaning of the apparent free or undefined variable.

2. In the actual system this is handled by an FSUBR rather than as the separate special case as shown here.

If the variable is bound several times on the a-list, only the first or most recent occurrence is changed. If the current binding of the variable is at a higher level than the entrance to the prog, then the change will remain in effect throughout the scope of that binding, and the old value will be lost.

If the variable does not occur on the a-list, then error diagnostic A4 or A5 will occur.

4. When a return is encountered at any point, its argument is evaluated and returned as the value of the most recent prog that has been entered.

5. The form go may be used only in two ways.

a. (GO X) may occur on the top level of the prog. x must be a location symbol of this prog and not another one on a higher or lower level.

b. This form may also occur as one of the value parts of a conditional expression, if this conditional expression occurs on the top level of the prog.

If a go is used incorrectly or refers to a nonexistent location, error diagnostic A6 will occur.

6. When the form cond occurs on the top level of a prog, it differs from other conds in the following ways.

a. It is the only instance in which a go can occur inside a cond.

b. If the cond runs out of clauses, error diagnostic A3 will not occur. Instead, the prog will continue with the next statement.

7. When a statement is executed, this has the following meaning, with the exception of the special forms cond, go, return, setq and the pseudo-function set, all of which are peculiar to prog.

The statement s is executed by performing eval[s;a], where a is the current a-list, and then ignoring the value.

8. If a prog runs out of statements, its value is NIL.

When a prog is compiled, it will have the same effect as when it is interpreted, although the method of execution is much different; for example, a go is always compiled as a transfer. The following points should be noted concerning declared variables.[1]

1. Program variables follow the same rules as λ variables do.

a. If a variable is purely local, it need not be declared.

b. Special variables can be used as free variables in compiled functions. They may be set at a lower level than that at which they are bound.

c. Common program variables maintain complete communication between compiled programs and the interpreter.

2. set as distinct from setq can only be used to set common variables.

---

1. See Appendix D for an explanation of variable declaration.

APPENDIX C

THE LISP ASSEMBLY PROGRAM (LAP)

lap is a two-pass assembler. It was specifically designed for use by the new compiler, but it can also be used for defining functions in machine language, and for making
patches.

lap is an entirely internal assembler. Its input is in the form of an S-expression
that remains in core memory during the entire assembly. No input tape is moved during
the assembly. lap does not produce binary output in the form of cards. It assembles
directly into memory during the second pass.

Format

lap is a pseudo-function with two arguments. The first argument is the listing, the
second argument is the initial symbol table. The value of lap is the final symbol table.

The first item of the listing is always the origin. All remaining items of the listing
are either location symbols if they are atomic symbols other than NIL, or instructions
if they are composite S-expressions or if they are NIL.

Origin

The origin informs the assembler where the assembly is to start, and whether it
is to be made available as a LISP function. The origin must have one of the following
formats.

1. If the origin is an octal or decimal number, then the assembly starts at that
location.

2. If the origin is an atomic symbol other than NIL, then this symbol must have
a permanent value (SYM) on its property list. The value of this SYM is a number specifying the starting location.

3. If the origin is NIL, then the assembly will start in the first available location
in binary program space. If the assembly is successfully completed, then the cell specifying the first unused location in binary program space is updated. If the assembly
cannot fit in binary program space, an error diagnostic will be given.

4. If the origin is of the form (name type n), then the assembly is in binary program space as in the case above. When the assembly is completed, the indicator, type,
is placed on the property list of the atomic symbol name. Following the indicator is a
pointer to a word containing TXL, the first location of the program just assembled in
the address, and the number n in the decrement. type is usually either SUBR or
FSUBR. n is the number of arguments which the subroutine expects.

Symbols

Atomic symbols appearing on the listing (except NIL or the first item on the listing) are treated as location symbols. The appearance of the symbol defines it as the location of the next instruction in the listing. During pass one, these symbols and their values are made into a pair list, and appended to the initial symbol table to form the final symbol table. This is used in pass two to evaluate the symbols when they occur in instructions. It is also the value of _lap_.

Symbols occurring on this table are defined only for the current assembly. The symbol table is discarded after each assembly.

Permanent symbols are defined by putting the indicator SYM followed by a pointer to a value on their property lists.

Instructions

Each instruction is a list of from zero to four fields. Each field is evaluated in the same manner; however, the fields are combined as follows.

1. The first field is taken as a full word.

2. The second field is reduced algebraically modulo 2^{15}, and is OR'ed into the address part of the word. An arithmetic -1 is reduced to 77777Q.

3. The third field is shifted left 15 bits, and then OR'ed into the word. A tag of four is written "4". A tag of 2 in an instruction with indirect bits is written "602Q".

4. The fourth field is reduced modulo 2^{15} and is OR'ed into the decrement.

Fields

Fields are evaluated by testing for each of the following conditions in the order listed.

1. If the field is atomic.

   a. The atomic symbol NIL has for its value the contents of the cell $ORG. During an assembly that is not in binary program space, this cell contains the starting address of the next assembly to go into binary program space.

   b. The atomic symbol * has the current location as its value.

   c. The symbol table is searched for an atomic symbol that is identical to the field.

   d. If the field is a number, then its numerical value is used.

   e. The property list of the atomic field is searched for either a SYM, a SUBR, or an FSUBR.

2. If the field is of the form (E a), then the value of the field is the complement of the address of the S-expression a. The expression a is protected so that it can never be collected by the garbage collector.

3. If the field is of the form (QUOTE a), then a literal quantity containing a in the decrement is created. It is the address of this quantity that is assembled. Quoted S-expressions are protected against being collected by the garbage collector. A new literal will not be created if it is _equal_ to one that already exists.

4. If the field is of the form (SPECIAL x), then the value is the address of the SPECIAL cell on the property list of x. If one does not already exist, it will be created.

The SPECIAL cell itself (but not the entire atom) is protected against garbage collection.

5. In all other cases, the field is assumed to be a list of subfields, and their sum is taken. The subfields must be of types 1-4 above.

Error Diagnostics

L   1   Unable to determine origin. No assembly.

L   2   Out of binary program space. Second pass cancelled.

L   3   Undefined symbol. Assembly incomplete.

L   4   Type five field contains type five fields inside itself. Assembly incomplete.

Opdefine

opdefine is a pseudo-function for defining new quantities for LAP. It puts a SYM on the property list of the symbol that is being defined. Its argument is a list of pairs. Each pair is a symbol and its numerical value. Note that these pairs are not "dotted" pairs.

Example

```
OPDEFINE  ( (    (CLA 500Q8)
                 (TRA 2Q9)
                 (LOAD 1000)
                 (OVBGN 7432Q)  ) )
```

The following op-codes are defined in the standard system:

AXT	PXA	SUB	TRA
CLA	PXD	SXA	TSX
LDQ	STD	SXD	TXH
LXA	STO	TIX	TXI
LXD	STQ	TLQ	TXL
PAX	STR	TNX	TZE
PDX	STZ	TNZ	XCA

Examples of the Use of LAP

Example 1: A LISP function

The predicate greater induces an arbitrary canonical order among atomic symbols.

```
LAP ( (   (GREATER SUBR 2) (TLQ (* 3)) (PXA 0 0)
          (TRA 1 4) (CLA  (QUOTE *T* ) ) (TRA 1 4) )NIL)
```

Example 2: A patch

The instruction TSX 6204Q must be inserted after location 6217Q. 6217Q contains CLA 6243Q and this instruction must be moved to the patch.

```
LAP ( (6217Q (TRA NIL) )NIL)
LAP ( (NIL (CLA A) (TSX 6204Q) (TRA B) )
      ( (A · 6243Q)    (B · 6220Q) ) )
```

APPENDIX D
THE LISP COMPILER

The LISP Compiler is a program written in LISP that translates S-expression definitions of functions into machine language subroutines. It is an optional feature that
makes programs run many times faster than they would if they were to be interpreted
at run time by the interpreter.

When the compiler is called upon to compile a function, it looks for an EXPR or
FEXPR on the property list of the function name. The compiler then translates this
S-expression into an S-expression that represents a subroutine in the LISP Assembly
Language (LAP). LAP then proceeds to assemble this program into binary program
space. Thus an EXPR, or an FEXPR, has been changed to a SUBR or an FSUBR,
respectively.

Experience has shown that compiled programs run anywhere from 10 to 100 times
as fast as interpreted programs, the time depending upon the nature of the program.
Compiled programs are also more economical with memory than their corresponding
S-expressions, taking only from 50 per cent to 80 per cent as much space.[1]

The major part of the compiler is a translator or function from the S-expression
function notation into the assembly language, LAP. The only reasons why the compiler
is regarded as a pseudo-function are that it calls LAP, and it removes EXPR's and
FEXPR's when it has finished compiling.

The compiler has an interesting and perhaps unique history. It was developed in
the following steps:

1. The compiler was written and debugged as a LISP program consisting of a set
of S-expression definitions of functions. Any future change or correction to the compiler must start with these definitions; therefore they are included in the LISP Library.

2. The compiler was commanded to compile itself. This operation is called bootstrapping. It takes more than 5 minutes on the IBM 7090 computer to do this, since
most parts of the compiler are being interpreted during most of this time.

3. To avoid having to repeat the slow bootstrapping operation each time a system
tape is created, the entire compiler was punched out in assembly language by using
punchlap.

4. When a system tape is to be made, the compiler in assembly language is read
in by using readlap.

The compiler is called by using the pseudo-function compile. The argument of compile is a list of the names of functions to be compiled. Each atomic symbol on this list
should have either an EXPR or an FEXPR on its property list before being compiled.

The processing of each function occurs in three steps. First, the S-expression for
the function is translated into assembly language. If no S-expression is found, then the
compiler will print this fact and proceed with the next function. Second, the assembly

---

1. Since the compiled program is placed in binary program space, which is normally
not otherwise accessible, one gains as free storage the total space formerly occupied
by the S-expression definition.

language program is assembled by LAP. Finally, if no error has occurred, then the EXPR or FEXPR is removed from the property list. When certain errors caused by undeclared free variables occur, the compiler will print a diagnostic and continue. This diagnostic will be spuriously produced when programs leaning on APVALs are compiled.

When writing a large LISP program, it is better to debug the individual function definitions by using the interpreter, and compile them only when they are known to work.

Persons planning to use the compiler should note the following points:

1. It is not necessary to compile all of the functions that are used in a particular run. The interpreter is designed to link with compiled functions. Compiled functions that use interpreted functions will call the interpreter to evaluate these at run time.

2. The order in which functions are compiled is of no significance. It is not even necessary to have all of the functions defined until they are actually used at run time. (Special forms are an exception to this rule. They must be defined before any function that calls them is compiled.)

3. If the form LABEL is used dynamically, the resulting function will not compile properly.

4. Free variables in compiled functions must be declared before the function is compiled. This is discussed at length in this appendix.

Excise

The compiler and the assembler LAP can be removed from the system by using the pseudo-function excise. If excise [NIL] is executed, then the compiler will be removed. If excise [*T*] is executed, then the compiler and LAP will both be excised. One may execute excise [NIL] and then excise [*T*] at a later time. When a portion of the system is excised, the region of memory that it occupied is converted into additional free-storage space.

Free Variables

A variable is bound in a particular function when it occurs in a list of bound variables following the word LAMBDA or PROG. Any variable that is not bound is free.

Example

```
(LAMBDA (A) (PROG (B)
 S   (SETQ B A)
     (COND ((NULL B) (RETURN C)))
     (SETQ C (CONS (CAR A) C))
     (GO S) ))
```

A and B are bound variables, C is a free variable.

When a variable is used free, it must have been bound by a higher level function. If a program is being run interpretively, and a free variable is used without having been bound on a higher level, error diagnostic *A 8* will occur.

77

If the program is being run compiled, the diagnostic may not occur, and the variable may have value NIL.

There are three types of variables in compiled functions: ordinary variables, SPECIAL variables, and COMMON variables. SPECIAL and COMMON variables must be declared before compiling. Any variable that is not declared will be considered an ordinary variable.

When functions are translated into subroutines, the concept of a variable is translated into a location where an argument is stored. If the variable is an ordinary one, then a storage location for it is set up on the push-down list. Other functions cannot find this private cell, making it impossible to use it as a free variable.

SPECIAL variables have the indicator SPECIAL on their property lists. Following the indicator there is a pointer to a fixed cell. When this variable is bound, the old value is saved on the push-down list, and the current value is stored in the SPECIAL cell. When it is no longer bound, the old value must be restored. When a function uses this variable free, then the quantity in the SPECIAL cell is picked up.

SPECIAL variables are declared by using the pseudo-function special[a], where a is a list of variable names. This sets up the SPECIAL indicator and creates a SPECIAL cell. Both the indicator and the cell can be removed by the pseudo-function unspecial[a], where a is a list of variable names. It is important that the declaration be in effect at compile time. It may be removed at run time.

The compiler refers to SPECIAL cells, using the LAP field (SPECIAL X) whose value is the address of the SPECIAL cell. When a variable has been declared, removed, and then declared again, a new cell is created and is actually a different variable.

SPECIAL variables are inexpensive and will allow free communication among compiled functions. They do not increase run time significantly. SPECIAL variables cannot be communicated between the interpreter and compiled functions.

COMMON variables have the flag COMMON on their property lists; however, this is only used to inform the compiler that they are COMMON, and is not needed at run time. COMMON variables are bound on an a-list by the compiled functions. When they are to be evaluated, eval is given this a-list. This happens at run time.

The use of COMMON variables will slow down any compiled function using them. However, they do provide complete communication between interpreted and compiled functions.

COMMON variables are declared by common[a], where a is a list of variable names. The declaration can be removed by uncommon[a], where a is a list of variable names.

Functional Constants

Consider the following definition of a function ydot by using an S-expression:

(YDOT (LAMBDA (X Y) (MAPLIST X (FUNCTION
    (LAMBDA (J) (CONS (CAR J) Y))))))

ydot[(A B C D);X]=[((A · X) (B · X) (C · X) (D · X))]

Following the word FUNCTION is a functional constant. If we consider it as a separate function, it is evident that it contains a bound variable "J", and a free variable "Y". This free variable must be declared SPECIAL or COMMON, even though it is bound in YDOT.

Functional Arguments

MAPLIST can be defined in S-expressions as follows:

```
(MAPLIST (LAMBDA (L FN) (COND
         ((NULL L) NIL)
         (T (CONS (FN L) (MAPLIST (CDR L) FN))) )))
```

The variable FN is used to bind a functional argument. That is, the value of FN is a function definition. This type of variable must be declared COMMON.

Link

Link is the routine that creates all linkage of compiled functions at run time.

The normal procedure for calling a compiled function is to place the arguments in the AC, MQ, $ARG3, ... and then to TSX FN,4. However, the first time any call is executed, there will be an STR in place of the TSX. The address and the decrement of the STR specify the name of the function that is being called, and the number of arguments that are being transmitted, respectively. The tag contains a 7. If there is no SUBR or FSUBR for the function that is being called, then link will call the interpreter that may find an EXPR or FEXPR. If there is a subroutine available, then link will form the instruction TSX and plant this on top of the STR.

Tracing Compiled Functions

trace will work for compiled functions, subject to the following restrictions.

1. The trace must be declared after the function has been compiled.

2. Once a direct TSX link is made, this particular calling point will not be traced. (Link will not make a TSX as long as the called function is being traced.)

79

APPENDIX E

OVERLORD - THE MONITOR

Overlord is the monitor of the LISP System. It controls the handling of tapes, the reading and writing of entire core images, the historical memory of the system, and the taking of dumps.

The LISP System uses 5 tape drives. They are listed here by name together with their customary addresses.

SYSTAP	Contains the System	B7
SYSTMP	Receives the Core Image	B3
SYSPIT	Punched Card Input	A2
SYSPOT	Printed Output	A3
SYSPPT	Punched Card Output	A4

The system tape contains a small bootstrap record with a loader, followed by a very long record that fills up almost all of the core memory of the machine.

The system is called by the two-card LISP loader which is placed in the on-line card reader. Octal corrections may be placed between the two cards of this loader. The format of these will be specified later.

The first loader card causes SYSTAP to be selected and the entire memory is immediately filled. Control then goes to a loader that reads octal correction cards until it recognizes the second loader card which is a binary transfer card to Overlord.

Overlord reads cards from the input looking for Overlord direction cards. Other cards are ignored except for the first one which is printed in the output.

Overlord cards either instruct the monitor to perform some specific function or else signal that a packet of doublets for evaluation is to follow immediately.

Before any packet is read, the entire system is read out onto SYSTMP. It is written in the same format as SYSTAP, and in fact is a copy of it. After each packet, one of two things may happen. Either a complete core image is read from SYSTMP, and thus memory is restored to the condition it was in before the packet was read, or the state of memory at the finish of the packet is read out onto SYSTMP. In the latter case, all function definitions and other memory changes are preserved.

Card Format

Octal correction cards can alter up to 4 words of memory per card. Each change specifies an address (5 octal digits) and a word to be placed there (12 octal digits). The card columns to use are as follows.

address	data word
2-6	7-18
20-24	25-36
38-42	43-54
56-60	61-72

Overlord cards have the Overlord direction beginning in column 8. If the card has no other field, then comments may begin in column 16. Otherwise, the other fields of the card begin in column 16 and are separated by commas. The comments may begin after the first blank past column 16.

Overlord Cards

TAPE   SYSPPT, B4

The TAPE Overlord card defines the actual drives to be assigned to the tapes. The system uses five tapes designated by the names SYSTAP, SYSTMP, SYSPIT, SYSPOT, and SYSPPT. The actual tape units may range from A0 through C9.

SIZE   N1, N2, N3, N4

The size card specifies the amount of storage to be allocated to binary program space, push-down, full words, and free storage in that order. The SIZE card must be used only once at the time when the system is created from a binary card deck. The fields are octal or decimal integers.

DUMP   L1, L2, 0

This Overlord card causes an octal dump of memory to be printed. The first two fields are octal or decimal integers specifying the range of the dump. The third field specifies the mode. 0 mode specifies a straight dump. 1 mode specifies that if the prefix and tag areas of a word are zero, then the complements of the address and decrement are dumped instead.

TEST

Specifies that a packet is to follow and that memory is to be restored from SYSTMP after the packet has been evaluated.

TST

Same as TEST

SET

The SET card specifies that a packet is to follow and that the memory state following the evaluation of the packet is to be set onto SYSTMP. If an error occurs during the evaluation of the packet, then the memory is to be restored from SYSTMP instead.

SETSET

The SETSET card is like SET except that it sets even if there has been an error.

DEBUG

This direction is like TEST except that after the doublets have been read in the entire object list is thrown away, making it impossible to do any further reading (except of numbers). This makes a considerable amount of free storage available but may cause trouble if certain atoms that are needed are not protected in some manner.

FIN

Causes the computer to halt. An end of file mark is written on SYSPOT. An end of file is written on SYSPPT only if it has been used. If the FIN card was read on-line, the computer halts after doing these things. If the FIN card came from SYSPIT, then

SYSPIT is advanced past the next end of file mark before the halt occurs.

Use of Sense Switches

1   Up—Input comes from SYSPIT.
     Down—Input comes from the card reader.

The loader cards and octal correction cards always go on-line.

3   Up—No effect
     Down—All output that is written onto either SYSPOT or SYSPPT will also appear
     on the on-line printer.

5   Up—No effect
     Down—Suppresses output normally written on SYSPOT and SYSPPT.

These switches are interrogated at the beginning of each record.

6   Up—The instruction STR will cause the interpreter to give error diagnostic F 5
     and continue with the next doublet.
     Down—The instruction STR will cause control to go to Overlord immediately.

The normal terminating condition of a LISP run is an HPR 77777, 7 with all bits of
AC and MQ filled with ones.   To return control to Overlord from this condition, push
RESET then START.

After a LISP run, the reel of tape that has been mounted on the SYSTMP drive has
become a system tape containing the basic system plus any changes that have been set
onto it.   It may be mounted on the SYSTAP drive for some future run to use definitions
that have been set onto it.

APPENDIX F

LISP INPUT AND OUTPUT

This appendix describes the LISP read and write programs and the character-manipulation programs. The read and write programs allow one to read and write S-expressions. The character-manipulating programs allow one to read and write individual characters, to process them internally, to break atomic symbols into their constituent characters, and to form atomic symbols from individual characters.

The actual input/output routines are identical for both the LISP read and write, and the character read and write. Input is always from either SYSPIT or the card reader. Printed output is always written on SYSPOT and/or the on-line printer. Punched output is always on SYSPPT and/or the on-line printer. The manner in which these choices are controlled was described in Appendix E.

LISP READ PRINT and PUNCH

The LISP read program reads S-expressions in the form of BCD characters and translates them into list structures. It recognizes the delimiters "("and")" and the separators "." "," and (blank). The comma and blank are completely equivalent.

An atomic symbol, when read in, is compared with existing atomic symbols. If it has not been encountered previously, a new atomic symbol with its property list is created. All atomic symbols except numbers and gensyms are on a list called the object list. This list is made of sublists called buckets. The atomic symbols are thrown into buckets by a hash process on their names. This speeds up the search that must occur during reading.

For the purpose of giving a more extended definition of an atomic symbol than was given in Section I, the 48 BCD characters are divided into the following categories.

     Class A   A B C ... Z = * /
     Class B   0 1 2 3 4 5 6 7 8 9 + − (11 punch)
     Class C   ( ) , . (blank)
     Class D $
     Class E   − (4-8 punch)

The 4–8 punch should not be used.

Symbols beginning with a Class B character are interpreted as numbers. Some sort of number conversion is attempted even if it does not make sense.

An ordinary atomic symbol is a sequence of up to 30 characters from classes A, B, and D, with the following restrictions.

    a. The first character must not be from class B.

    b. The first two characters must not be $ $.

    c. It must be delimited on either side by a character from class C.

There is a provision for reading in atomic symbols containing arbitrary characters.

This is done by punching the form $ $dsd, where s is any string of up to 30 characters, and d is any character not contained in the string s. Only the string s is used in forming the print name of the atomic symbol; d and the dollar signs will not appear when the atomic symbol is printed out.

Examples

Input	will print as
$ $XAX	A
$ $()))(	)))
$ $_UV.)_	UV.)
$ $/_./	_.

The operation of the read program is critically dependent upon the parsing of left and right parentheses. If an S-expression is deficient in one or more right parentheses, reading will continue into the next S-expression. An unmatched right parenthesis, or a dot that is out of context, will terminate reading and cause an error diagnostic.

The read program is called at the beginning of each packet to read doublets for evalquote until it comes to the S-expression STOP. read may also be used explicitly by the programmer. In this case, it will begin reading with the card following the STOP card because the read buffer is cleared by evalquote after the doublets and STOP have been read. After this, card boundaries are ignored, and one S-expression is read each time read is called. read has no arguments. Its value is the S-expression that it reads.

The pseudo-functions print and punch write one S-expression on the printed or punched output, respectively. In each case, the print or punch buffer is written out and cleared so that the next section of output begins on a new record.

prin1 is a pseudo-function that prints its argument, which must be an atomic symbol, and does not terminate the print line (unless it is full).

terpri prints what is left in the print buffer, and then clears it.

Characters and Character Objects

Each of the sixty-four 6-bit binary numbers corresponds to a BCD character, if we include illegal characters. Therefore, in order to manipulate these characters via LISP functions, each of them has a corresponding object. Of the 64 characters, 48 correspond to characters on the key punch, and the key-punch character is simply that character. The print names of the remaining characters will be described later. When a LISP function is described which has a character as either value or argument, we really mean that it has an object corresponding to a character as value or argument, respectively.

The first group of legal characters consists of the letters of the alphabet from A to Z. Each letter is a legitimate atomic symbol, and therefore may be referred to in a straightforward way, without ambiguity.

The second group of legal characters consists of the digits from 0 to 9. These must be handled with some care because if a digit is considered as an ordinary integer rather than a character a new nonunique object will be created corresponding to it, and this object will not be the same as the character object for the same digit, even though it has the same print name. Since the character-handling programs depend on the character objects being in specific locations, this will lead to error.

The read program has been arranged so that digits 0 through 9 read in as the corresponding character objects. These may be used in arithmetic just as any other number but, even though the result of an arithmetic operation lies between 0 and 9, it will not point to the corresponding character object. Thus character objects for 0 through 9 may be obtained only by reading them or by manipulation of print names.

The third group of legal characters is the special characters. These correspond to the remaining characters on the key punch, such as "$" and "=". Since some of these characters are not legitimate atomic symbols, there is a set of special character-value objects which can be used to refer to them.

A typical special character-value object, say DOLLAR, has the following structure

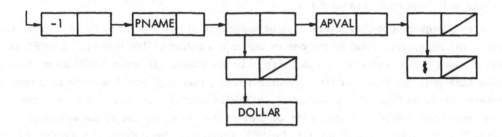

Thus "DOLLAR" has value "$".

The special character value objects and their permanent values are:

DOLLAR	$
SLASH	/
LPAR	(
RPAR	)
COMMA	,
PERIOD	.
PLUSS	+
DASH	– (11 punch)
STAR	*
BLANK	blank
EQSIGN	=

The following examples illustrate the use of their objects and their raison d'être. Each example consists of a doublet for evalquote followed by the result.

Examples

EVAL (DOLLAR NIL) value is "$"
EVAL ((PRINT PERIOD) NIL) value is "." and "." is also printed.

The remaining characters are all illegal as far as the key punch is concerned. The two characters corresponding to 12 and 72 have been reserved for end-of-file and end-of-record, respectively. The end-of-file character has print name EOF and the end-of-record character has print name EOR; corresponding to these character objects are two character value objects EOR and EOF, whose values are EOR and EOF respectively. The rest of the illegal character objects have print names corresponding to their octal representations preceded by $IL and followed by $. For instance, the character 77 corresponds to a character object with print name $IL77$.

The character objects are arranged in the machine so that their first cells occupy successive storage locations. Thus it is possible to go from a character to the corresponding object or conversely by a single addition or subtraction. This speeds up character-handling considerably, because it isn't necessary to search property lists of character objects for their print names; the names may be deduced from the object locations.

Packing and Unpacking Characters

When a sequence of characters is to be made into either a print name or a numerical object, the characters must be put one by one into a buffer called BOFFO. BOFFO is used to store the characters until they are to be combined. It is not available explicitly to the LISP programmer, but the character-packing functions are described in terms of their effects on BOFFO. At any point, BOFFO contains a sequence of characters. Each operation on BOFFO either adds another character at the end of the sequence or clears BOFFO, i.e., sets BOFFO to the null sequence. The maximum length of the sequence is 120 characters; an attempt to add more characters will cause an error.

The character-packing functions are:

1. pack [c]   :   SUBR   pseudo-function

    The argument of pack must be a character object. pack adds the character c at the end of the sequence of characters in BOFFO. The value of pack is NIL.

2. clearbuff [ ]   :   SUBR   pseudo-function

    clearbuff is a function of no arguments. It clears BOFFO and has value NIL. The contents of BOFFO are undefined until a clearbuff has been performed.

3. mknam [ ]   :   SUBR   pseudo-function

    mknam is a function of no arguments. Its value is a list of full words containing the characters in BOFFO in packed BCD form. The last word is filled out with the illegal character code 77 if necessary. After mknam is performed, BOFFO is automatically cleared. Note that intern [mknam[ ]] yields the object whose print name is in BOFFO.

4. numob [ ]   :   SUBR   pseudo-function

    numob is a function of no arguments. Its value is the numerical object represented by the sequence of characters in BOFFO. (Positive decimal integers from 0 to 9 are converted so as to point to the corresponding character object.)

5. <u>unpack</u> [x]:   :   SUBR   pseudo-function

      This function has as argument a pointer to a full word. <u>unpack</u> considers
the full word to be a set of 6 BCD characters, and has as value a list of these
characters ignoring all characters including and following the first 77.

6. <u>intern</u>[pname]   :   SUBR   pseudo-function

      This function has as argument a pointer to a PNAME type structure such as –

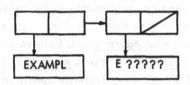

      Its value is the atomic symbol having this print name. If it does not already
exist, then a new atomic symbol will be created.

The Character-Classifying Predicates

1. <u>liter</u> [c]:   :   SUBR   predicate

      <u>liter</u> has as argument a character object. Its value is T if the character
is a letter of the alphabet, and F otherwise.

2. <u>digit</u> [c]:   :   SUBR   predicate

      <u>digit</u> has as argument a character object. Its value is T if the character
is a digit between 0 and 9, and F otherwise.

3. <u>opchar</u> [c]:   :   SUBR   predicate

      <u>opchar</u> has as argument a character object. Its value is T if the character
is +, –, /, *, or =, and F otherwise. <u>opchar</u> treats both minus signs equiva-
lently.

4. <u>dash</u> [c]:   :   SUBR   predicate

      <u>dash</u> has as argument a character object. Its value is T if the character
is either an 11-punch minus or an 8-4 punch minus, and F otherwise.

The Character-Reading Functions

      The character-reading functions make it possible to read characters one by one from
input.

      There is an object CURCHAR whose value is the character most recently read (as
an object). There is also an object CHARCOUNT whose value is an integer object giving
the column just read on the card, i. e., the column number of the character given by
CURCHAR. There are three functions which affect the value of CURCHAR:

1. <u>startread</u> [ ]:   :   SUBR   pseudo-function

      <u>startread</u> is a function of no arguments which causes a new card to be read.
The value of <u>startread</u> is the first character on that card, or more precisely,

the object corresponding to the first character on the card. If an end-of-file condition exists, the value of startread is EOF. The value of CURCHAR becomes the same as the output of startread, and the value of CHARCOUNT becomes 1. Both CURCHAR and CHARCOUNT are undefined until a startread is performed. A startread may be performed before the current card has been completely read.

2. advance [ ]:   :   SUBR   pseudo-function

    advance is a function of no arguments which causes the next character to be read. The value of advance is that character. After the 72nd character on the card has been read, the next advance will have value EOR. After reading EOR, the next advance will act like a startread, i.e., will read the first character of the next card unless an end-of-file condition exists. The new value of CURCHAR is the same as the output of advance; executing advance also increases the value of CHARCOUNT by 1. However, CHARCOUNT is undefined when CURCHAR is either EOR or EOF.

3. endread [ ]:   :   SUBR   pseudo-function

    endread is a function of no arguments which causes the remainder of the card to be read and ignored. endread sets CURCHAR to EOR and leaves CHARCOUNT undefined; the value of endread is always EOR. An advance following endread acts like a startread. If CURCHAR already has value EOR and endread is performed, CURCHAR will remain the same and endread will, as usual, have value EOR.

Diagnostic Function

error1 [ ]:   :   SUBR   pseudo-function

    error1 is a function of no arguments and has value NIL. It should be executed only while reading characters from a card (or tape). Its effect is to mark the character just read, i.e., CURCHAR, so that when the end of the card is reached, either by successive advances or by an endread, the entire card is printed out along with a visual pointer to the defective character. For a line consisting of ABCDEFG followed by blanks, a pointer to C would look like this:

V
ABCDEFG
A

If error1 is performed an even number of times on the same character, the A will not appear. If error1 is performed before the first startread or while CURCHAR has value EOR or EOF, it will have no effect. Executing a startread before the current card has been completed will cause the error1 printout to be lost. The card is considered to have been completed when CURCHAR has been set to EOR. Successive endreads will cause the error1 printout to be reprinted. Any number of characters in a given line may be marked by error1 .

APPENDIX G

MEMORY ALLOCATION AND THE GARBAGE COLLECTOR

The following diagram shows the way in which space is allocated in the LISP System.

77777	Loader
77600	LAP
	Compiler
70000	
	Free Storage
	Full Words
	Push-Down List
	Binary Program Space
17000	
	Interpreter, I/O, Read Print, Arithmetic, Overlord, Garbage Collector, and other system coding
00000	

The addresses in this chart are only approximate. The available space is divided among binary program space, push-down list, full-word space, and free-storage space as specified on the SIZE card when the system is made.

When the compiler and LAP are not to be used again, they may be eliminated by executing the pseudo-function <u>excise</u>. This part of the memory is then converted into free storage.

Free storage is the area in the computer where list structures are stored. This includes the property lists of atomic symbols, the definitions of all EXPR's and FEXPR's, evalquote doublets waiting to be executed, APVAL's, and partial results of the computation that is in progress.

Full-word space is filled with the BCD characters of PNAME's, the actual numbers of numerical atomic structures, and the TXL words of SUBR's, FSUBR's, and SYM's.

All available words in the free-storage area that are not in use are strung together in one long list called the free-storage list. Every time a word is needed (for example, by cons) the first word on the free-storage list is used, and the free-storage list is set to cdr of what it formerly was.

Full-word space is handled in the same way. No use is made of consecutive storage in either of these areas of memory. They are both scrambled.

When either of these lists is exhausted in the middle of a computation, the garbage collector is called automatically. Unless the computation is too large for the system, there are many words in free storage and full-word space that are no longer needed. The garbage collector locates these by marking those words that are needed. In free storage, the sign bit is used for marking. In full-word space, there is no room in the word itself. Marking is done in a bit table which is next to full-word space.

Since it is important that all needed lists be marked, the garbage collector starts marking from several base positions including the following:

1. The object list that includes all atomic symbols except numbers and generated names. This protects the atomic symbols, and all S-expressions that hang on the property lists of atomic symbols.

2. The portion of the push-down list that is currently being used. This protects partial results of the computation that is in progress.

3. The temlis, which is a list of registers scattered throughout the memory where binary programs store list structures that must be protected.

Marking proceeds as follows. If the cell is in full-word space, then the bit table is marked. If the cell is in free storage, then the sign is set minus, and car and cdr of the cell are marked. If the cell is anywhere else, then nothing is done.

After the marking is done, the new available word lists are made by stringing all unmarked words together. Finally, the signs in free storage are set plus.

A garbage collection takes approximately 1 second on the IBM 7090 computer. It can be recognized by the stationary pattern of the MQ lights. Any trap that prevents completion of a garbage collection will create a panic condition in memory from which there is no recovery.

APPENDIX H

RECURSION AND THE PUSH-DOWN LIST

One of the most powerful resources of the LISP language is its ability to accept function definitions that make use of the very function that is being defined. This may come about either directly by using the name of the function, or indirectly through a chain of function definitions that eventually return to the original ones. A definition of this type is called recursive. Its power lies in its ability to define an algorithm in terms of itself.

A recursive definition always has the possibility of not terminating and of being infinitely regressive. Some recursive definitions may terminate when given certain inputs and not terminate for others. It is theoretically impossible to determine whether a definition will terminate in the general case; however, it is often possible to show that particular cases will or will not terminate.

LISP is designed in such a way that all functions for which the possibility of recursion can exist are in fact recursive. This requires that all temporary stored results related to the computation that is in progress be set aside when a piece of coding is to be used recursively, and that they be later restored. This is done automatically and need not be programmed explicitly.

All saving of temporary results in LISP is performed on a linear block of storage called the push-down list. Each set of stored data that is moved onto the push-down list is in a block labeled with its size and the name of the subroutine from which it came. Since it is in the nature of recursion that the first block to be saved is always the last block to be restored, it is possible to keep the push-down list compact.

The frontier of the push-down list can always be found by referring to the cell CPPI. The decrement of this cell contains the complementary address of the first available unused location on the push-down list. Index register 1 also contains this quantity, except during certain nonrecursive subroutines; in these last cases it must be restored upon leaving these routines.

There are two types of blocks to be found on the push-down list, those put there by SAVE, and those put there by *MOVE. SAVE blocks are moved from fixed locations in certain subroutines onto the push-down list, and then moved back to the place where they came from by UNSAVE. Each block contains parameters that tell UNSAVE how many words are to be moved, and where they are to be moved to.

Functions compiled by the LISP compiler do not make use of storage cells located near the actual programming. All data are stored directly on the push-down list and referenced by using index register 1. *MOVE is used to update CPPI and index register 1, to place the arguments on the push-down list, and to set up the parameters for the push-down block.

Because pointers to list structures are normally stored on the push-down list, the garbage collector must mark the currently active portion of the push-down list during a garbage collection. Sometimes quantities are placed on the push-down list which should not be marked. In this case, the sign bit must be negative. Cells on the active portion of the push-down list having a negative sign bit will not be marked.

When an error occurs, an examination of the push-down list is an excellent indication of what was occurring at the time of the error. Since each block on the push-down list has the name of the function to which it belongs, it is possible to form a list of these names. This is called the backtrace, and is normally printed out after error diagnostics.

LISP FOR SHARE DISTRIBUTION

The Artificial Intelligence Project at Stanford University has produced a version of LISP 1.5 to be distributed by SHARE. In the middle of February 1965 the system is complete and is available from Stanford. The system should be available from SHARE by the end of March 1965.

SHARE LISP differs somewhat from the LISP 1.5 system described in the LISP 1.5 Programmer's Manual, but only in (generally) inessential details. It is hoped that the changes will be widely hailed as improvements.

Verbos and the Garbage Collector

The garbage collector now prints its message in a single-spaced format; thus, the amount of paper generated by a program with many cons'es is somewhat less than formerly. Furthermore, the garbage collector printout may be suspended by executing "VERBOS(NIL)"; and the printout may be reinstated by executing "VERBOS(*T*)".

Flap Trap

Every now and then a state of affairs known as floating-point trap occurs — this results when a floating-point arithmetic instruction generates a number whose exponent is too large in magnitude for the eight-bit field reserved for it. When this trap occurs and the offending exponent is negative, the obvious thing to do is to call the result zero. The old system, however, simply printed out a "FLAP TRAP" error message and went on to the next pair of S-expressions to be evaluated. The new system stores a floating-point zero in the accumulator when an underflow occurs. (There has, as yet, been no request to have "infinity" stored in the accumulator when an overflow occurs.)

Time

The new system prints the time upon entering and leaving evalquote. In fact, two times are printed, but in a neat, concise, impersonal manner which, it is felt, is more suitable to the "age of automation" than the quote from Lewis Carroll. The times are printed in minutes and milliseconds; the first time is the age of the packet — by definition, this is zero when evalquote is first entered — and the second time is the age of the system being used. Thus, when evalquote is left, the time printout tells how much time was spent in the execution of the packet and how much time has been spent in execution of SET or SETSET packets since the birth of the system plus the time spent in the packet being finished. This time printout, to be meaningful, requires the computer to have a millisecond clock in cell 5 (RPQ F 89349, with millisecond feature).

It is also possible to determine how much time is required to execute a given function. "TIME1( )" initializes two time cells to zero and prints out, in the same format that is used for the evalquote time printout, two times, and these are both zero. "TIME()" prints (again in the evalquote time printout format) the time since the last execution of "TIME()" and the time since the last execution of "TIME1()". The use of the time and timel functions has no effect on the times recorded by evalquote.

Lap and Symtab

Heretofore, lap has not only returned the symbol table as its value but has printed it out as well. This phenomenon is familiar to those who have much at all to do with lap or the compiler. The lap in the new system always prints the function name and the octal location in which the first word of the assembled function is stored. (If the assembled function is not a SUBR or FSUBR, then only the octal origin of the assembled code is printed.) The printout is left-justified on the output page and has the form "⟨function name⟩ (ORIGIN xxxxxQ)".

The value of lap is still the symbol table, but the printing of the symbol table may be suspended by executing "SYMTAB(NIL)"; and the printing may be restored by executing "SYMTAB(*T*)".

Non-Printing Compiler

The problem of the verbosity of the compiler is only slightly abated by the symtab function. The remainder of the trouble may be cured by executing "LISTING(NIL)". This turns off the printout of the lap code generated by the compiler. And, of course, the printout may be reinstated by executing "LISTING(*T*)". Thus, for a perfectly quiet compilation (except for the origin printout by lap), one need only execute "SYMTAB(NIL)" and "LISTING(NIL)" before compiling.

Tracecount (Alarm-Clock Trace)

The trace feature of LISP is quite useful; but, with very little encouragement, it can be made to generate wastebaskets full of useless output. Often a programmer will find that his output (without tracing) consists of many lines of garbage collector printout, an error message, and a few cryptic remarks concerning the condition of the push-down list at the time the error occurred. In such a situation, one wishes he could begin tracing only a short time before the occurrence of the error. The tracecount function permits exactly this. "TRACECOUNT(x)" causes the tracing (of those functions designated to be traced by the trace function call) to begin after x number of function entrances. Furthermore, when the tracecount mechanism has been activated, by execution of "TRACECOUNT(x)", some of the blank space in the garbage collector printout will be used to output the number of function entrances which have taken place up to the time of the garbage collection; each time

94

the arguments or value of a traced function are printed the number of function entrances will be printed; and if an error occurs, the number of function entrances accomplished before the error will be printed.

The tracecount feature (or alarm-clock trace, as it is called by Marvin Minsky of M. I. T.) enables a programmer to run a job (preceding the program by "TRACECOUNT(0)"), estimate the number of function entrances that occur before the program generates an error condition or a wrong answer, and then run the job again, tracing only the pertinent portion of the execution.

Space and Eject

A small amount of additional control over the form of the data printed by LISP has been provided in the space and eject functions.

"SPACE(*T*)" causes all output to be double-spaced. "SPACE(NIL)" restores the spacing to its original status; in particular, the output of the print routine reverts to single-spacing, and the "END OF EVALQUOTE OPERATOR" printout again ejects the page before printing.

"EJECT()" causes a blank line with a carriage control character of 1 to be printed on the output tape. The result is a skip to the top of the next page of output.

Untime

This routine is not available to the programmer, but its mention here may prevent some anxiety. In the event that the program time estimate is exceeded during system I/O, using the old system, one finds himself in the position of having part of one system and part of another stored in core or on the SYSTMP. This situation would be intolerable if the programmer were trying to save some definitions so that he could use them later. To avoid this unpleasantness, the system I/O routines have been modified so that the clock is, in essence, turned off during system I/O and three seconds is automatically added to the elapsed time at the conclusion of the read or write operation (in a machine with a millisecond core clock this is the case — machines with 1/60 second core clocks add 50 seconds, but this is easily changed). A clock trap that would normally have occurred during the execution of the read or write will be executed before the I/O operation takes place.

Tape

A few programmers with very large programs have long bemoaned the inability of LISP to communicate between different systems. The functions tape, rewind, mprint, mread, and backspace have been designed to alleviate this difficulty. "TAPE(s)", where s is a list, allows the user to specify up to ten scratch tapes; if more than ten are specified, only the first ten are used. The value of tape is its argument. The initial tape settings are, from one to ten, A4, A5, A6, A7, A8, B2,

B3, B4, B5, B6. The tapes must be specified by the octal number that occurs in the address portion of a machine-language instruction to rewind that tape; that is, a four-digit octal number is required — the first (high-order) digit is a 1 if channel A is desired, 2 if channel B is desired; the second digit must be a 2; the third and fourth are the octal representation of the unit number. Thus, to specify that scratch tapes one, two, and three are to be tapes A4, B1, and A5, respectively, execute "TAPE ((1204Q 2201Q 1205Q))". Only the low-order fifteen bits of the numbers in the tape list are used by the tape routines, so it is possible to use decimal integers or floating-point numbers in the tape list without generating errors.

Rewind

"REWIND(x)" rewinds scratch tape x, as specified in the most recently executed tape function. For example, if the last tape function executed was "TAPE ((1204Q 2201Q))", then "REWIND(2)" will cause tape B1 to be rewound. The value of rewind is NIL.

Mprint

"MPRINT(x s)" prints the S-expression s on scratch tape x. The format of the output is identical to the normal LISP output, except that sequence numbers are printed in the rightmost eight columns of the output line and the output line is only 80 characters long (the scratch tape output is generated by the punch routine), and is suitable for punching or being read by mread. The value of mprint is the list printed.

Mread

"MREAD(x)" reads one S-expression from scratch tape x. The value of mread is the S-expression read.

Backspace

"BACKSPACE(x)" causes scratch tape x to be backspaced one record. Caution in the use of this function is recommended, for if an S-expression to be read from tape contains more than 72 characters, then it will occupy more than one record on the tape, and single backspace will not move the tape all the way back to the beginning of the S-expression. The value of backspace is NIL.

Evalquote

Evalquote is available to the programmer as a LISP function — thus, one may now write "(EVALQUOTE APPEND ((A)(B C D)))", rather than "(EVAL (QUOTE (APPEND (A)(B C D))) NIL)", should one desire to do so.

Backtrace

This function was copied (not quite literally) from M. I. T.'s LISP system on the time-shared 7094. <u>Backtrace</u> is a function of no arguments in which the manner of specifying the no arguments constitutes, in effect, an argument. The first call of <u>backtrace</u>, with any argument, or with none, suspends backtrace printouts when errors occur. Thereafter, the value of "BACKTRACE NIL" is the backtrace for the most recent error; and "BACKTRACE x", for x not NIL, restores the backtrace printout to the error routine. <u>Backtrace</u> should always be evaluated by <u>evalquote</u>.

Read-In Errors

A common cause of free-storage or circular list printouts is an error (in parenthesis count, usually) during the initial read-in of a packet. The new system causes the accumulator to be cleared if an error occurs during the initial read-in, so that the contents of the accumulator are printed as "NIL".

Obkeep

Anyone desperate for a few more words of free storage may make up a list, s, of all atom names he wants to retain in his personal LISP systems, then execute (in a SET packet) "OBKEEP(s)". All atoms except those which are members of s will be eliminated from the object list.

Reserved

"RESERVED NIL" prints the names of the atoms on the object list in alphabetical order, along with the indicators (not alphabetized, and flags may be missed) on their property lists. This function should help to solve some of the problems that arise involving mysterious behavior of compiled functions that worked fine when interpreted.

Gensym and Symnam

<u>Gensym</u> now omits leading zeroes from the numeric portions of the print-names of the symbols it generates; thus, what once looked like "G00001" now prints as "G1". Furthermore, it is possible to specify a heading word of from zero to six characters for the <u>gensym</u> symbols by executing <u>symnam</u>. "SYMNAM(NIL)" causes LISP-generated symbols to have purely numeric print-names (but they are not numbers). The numeric portions of the print-names are truncated from the left so as not to overlap the heading characters. Thus, "SYMNAM(AAAAA)" causes <u>gensym</u> to produce distinct atoms with the following (not necessarily distinct) print-names: AAAAA1, AAAAA2, . . ., AAAAA9, AAAAA0, AAAAA1, ... The argument of <u>symnam</u> must have the indicator PNAME on its property list. "SYMNAM(12)" will cause undefined results.

If

For the convenience of those who find it difficult to get along with the "COND" form of the conditional statement, the following "IF" forms are provided in the new system. "IF (a THEN b ELSE c)" and "IF (a b c)" are equivalent to "COND ((a b)(T c))". "IF (a THEN b)" and "IF (a b)" are equivalent to "COND ((a b))".

For

"FOR (index i s u d_1 . . . d_n)", for n less than 17, sets index to the value of i and skips out of the following loop as soon as the value of u is not NIL: evaluate u, evaluate d_1, . . ., evaluate d_n, evaluate s, go to the beginning of the loop. If i, s, and u are numbers, then the for statement is similar to the ALGOL "for index = i step s until u do begin d_1 . . . d_n end". The value of the for statement is the value of d_n the last time it was evaluated. The final value of index is available outside the for function because cset is used to set the index.

Sublis

Sublis has been re-hand-compiled so that it behaves as if it were defined as follows:

```
sublis[p;e] =
    label[suba;lambda[[e];[
      atom[e] →
        label[subb;lambda[[x];[
          null[x] → e;
          eq[caar[x];e] → cdar[x];
          T → subb[cdr[x]]
        ]]][p];
      T →
        lambda[[u;v];[
          and[equal[car[e];u];equal[cdr[e];v]] → e;
          T → cons[u;v]
        ]][suba[car[e]];suba[cdr[e]]]
    ]]][e].
```

The differences between the new sublis and the old one, as far as the programmer is concerned, are that the new model is faster and the result shares as much storage as possible with e.

Characteristics of the System

The set-up deck supplied with the SHARE LISP system produces a system tape with the following properties:

Size (in words) —

    Binary Program Space 14000 octal

    Push-Down List 5000 octal

    Full-Word Space 4220 octal

    Free Storage 22400 octal

System Tape (SYSTAP) B7

System Temporary Tape (SYSTMP) B6

System Input Tape (SYSPIT) A2

System Output Tape (SYSPOT) A3

System Punch Tape (SYSPPT) A3

The console switches may be used to obtain special results:

    SW1 on for LISP input from on-line card reader

    SW2 has no effect

    SW3 on for LISP output on on-line printer

    SW4 has no effect

    SW5 on to suppress SYSPOT output

    SW6 on to return to overlord after accumulator printout resulting from
        error *F 5*.   SW6 off for error printout.

INDEX TO FUNCTION DESCRIPTIONS

INDEX TO FUNCTION DESCRIPTIONS

INDEX TO FUNCTION DESCRIPTIONS

GLOSSARY

Symbol or Term	Definition
Algol 60	An international standard programming language for describing numerical computation.
algorithm	A procedure that is unambiguous and sufficiently mechanized so as to be programmable on a computer.
a-list	A synonym for association list.
assembly program	A program that translates from a symbolic instruction language such as FAP or LAP into the language of a machine. The statements in an assembly language, with few exceptions, are one to one with the machine language instructions to which they translate. Unlike machine language, an assembly language allows the programmer to use symbols with mnemonic significance. LISP was written in the assembly language, FAP. LISP contains a small internal assembly program, LAP.
association list	A list of pairs of terms which is equivalent to a table with two columns. It is used to pair bound variables with their values. Example: ((VAR1 . VAL1) (B . (U V (W))) (C . Z))
atom	A synonym for atomic symbol.
atomic symbol	The basic constituent of an S-expression. The legal atomic symbols are certain strings of letters, digits, and special characters defined precisely in Appendix F. Examples: A NIL ATOM A1 METHIMPIKEHOSES
back trace	A list of the names of functions that have been entered but not completed at the time when an error occurs.
basic functions: car, cdr, cons, eq and atom	These functions are called basic because the entire class of computable functions of S-expressions can be built from them by using composition, conditional expressions, and recursion.
Boolean form	The special forms involving AND, OR, and NOT, which can be used to build up propositional expressions.
bound variable	A variable included in the list of bound variables after LAMBDA is bound within the scope of the LAMBDA. This means that its value is the argument corresponding in position to the occurrence of the variable in the LAMBDA list. For example, in an expression of the form ((LAMBDA (X Y) ε) (QUOTE (A . B)) (QUOTE C)), X has the value (A . B) and Y the value C at any of their occurrences in ε.
compiler	A program that translates from a source language into machine (or assembly) language. Unlike most compilers, the LISP compiler does not need to compile an entire program before execution. It can compile individual functions defined by S-expressions into machine language during a run.

103

GLOSSARY

Symbol or Term	Definition
composition	To compose a function is to use the value of one function as an argument for another function. This is usually written with nested brackets or parentheses. Examples: cons[car[x];cdr[y]], or as an S-expression (CONS (CAR X) (CDR Y)); and a+(b·(c+d)).
conditional expression	An expression containing a list of propositional expressions and corresponding forms as values. The value is the value of the entire conditional expression. Examples of different notations for conditional expression: M-expression: [a<0→b;T→C] S-expression: (COND ((LESSP A 0) B) (T C)) Algol 60: if a<0 then b else c.
constant	A symbol whose value does not change during a computation. For example, the value of F is always NIL, and the value of 5 is always 5. Other constants in the LISP system are described in Appendix A under the heading "APVAL."
dot notation	A method of writing S-expressions by combining only pairs of S-expressions rather than lists of indefinite length. The dot notation is the fundamental notation of LISP. The list notation is defined in terms of the dot notation.
doublet	A pair of arguments for evalquote, the LISP interpreter.
flag	An item on the property list of an atomic symbol. A flag is not followed by a value as an indicator is. TRACE and COMMON are flags.
form	An expression that may be evaluated when some correspondence has been set up between the variables contained in it and a set of actual arguments. The important distinction between functions and forms is treated in section 1.4.
free-storage list	The list of available words in the free storage of the computer memory. Each time a cons is performed the first word on the free-storage list is removed. When the free-storage list is exhausted, a new one is created by the garbage collector.
free variable	A variable that is neither a program variable nor a bound variable. A variable can be considered bound or free only within the context in which it appears. If a variable is to be evaluated by the interpreter, it must be bound at some level or have a constant value or an assigned value. For definitions covering these three cases see bound variable, program variable, and constant.
functional	A function that can have functions as arguments. apply, eval, maplist, search, and sassoc are functionals in LISP.

GLOSSARY

Symbol or Term	Definition
functional argument	A function that is an argument for a functional. In LISP, a functional argument is quoted by using the special form (FUNCTION fn*).
garbage collector	The routine in LISP which identifies all active list structure by tracing it from fixed base cells and marking it, and then collects all unneeded cells (garbage) into a free-storage list so that these words can be used again.
indicator	An atomic symbol occurring on a property list that specifies that the next item on the list is a certain property. Unlike a flag, an indicator always has a property following it. SPECIAL, EXPR, FSUBR, and APVAL are examples of indicators.
interpreter	An interpreter executes a source-language program by examining the source language and performing the specified algorithms. This is in contrast to a translator or compiler which translates a source-language program into machine language for subsequent execution. LISP has both an interpreter and a compiler.
lambda notation	The notation first used by Church for converting forms into names of functions. A form in $a_2, \ldots, a_n$ is turned into the function of n variables whose arguments are in order a_i by writing $\lambda[[a_1 \ldots a_n];\text{form}]$
list	An S-expression satisfying the predicate $$\text{listp}[x] = \text{null}[x] \lor [\text{not}[\text{atom}[x]] \land \text{listp}[\text{cdr}[x]]]$$ An S-expression of this form can be written $(m_1, m_2, \ldots m_n)$, which stands for the dot-notation expression $(m_1 \cdot (m_2 \cdot \ldots (m_n \cdot \text{NIL}) \ldots))$.
list notation	A method of writing S-expressions by using the form $(m_1, m_2, \ldots, m_n)$ to stand for the dot-notation expression $(m_1 \cdot (m_2 \cdot \ldots (m_n \cdot \text{NIL}) \ldots))$
logical form	See Boolian form
M-expression	An expression in the LISP language for writing functions of S-expressions. M-expressions cannot be read by the machine at present but must be hand-translated into S-expressions.
object	A synonym for atomic symbol.
Overlord	The monitor and system tape-handling section of the LISP system.
packet	A sequence of doublets for the interpreter. Each packet is preceded by an Overlord control card and ends with the word STOP.

GLOSSARY

Symbol or Term	Definition
partial function	A function that is defined for only part of its normal domain. It may not be possible to decide exactly for which arguments the function is defined because, for such arguments, the computation may continue indefinitely.
pointer	In LISP the complement of the address of a word is called a pointer to that word.
predicate	A function whose value is <u>true</u> or <u>false</u>. In LISP <u>true</u> and <u>false</u> are represented by the atomic symbols *T* and NIL. The symbols T and F have *T* and NIL as values.
program variable	A variable that is declared in the list of variables following the word PROG. Program variables have initially the value NIL, but they can be assigned arbitrary S-expressions as values by using SET or SETQ.
property	An expresssion or quantity associated with an atomic symbol. It is found on the property list preceded by an indicator.
property list	The list structure associated with an atomic symbol containing its print name and other properties, such as its value as a constant or its definition as a function.
propositional expression	An expression that is <u>true</u> or <u>false</u> when evaluated. The relation between propositional expressions and predicates is exactly the same as the relation between form and function.
pseudo-function	A program that is called as if it were a function, but has effects other than that of delivering its value. For example, PRINT, READ, RPLACA.
push-down list	The last-in-first-out memory area for saving partial results of recursive functions.
reclaimer	A synonym for the garbage collector.
recursion	The technique of defining an algorithm in terms of itself.
special form	A form having an indefinite number of arguments and/or arguments that are understood as being quoted before being given to the special form to evaluate.
trace	A debugging aid that causes a notice to be printed of every occurrence of an entry to or exit from any of the specified functions, with its appropriate arguments or value.
translator	A program whose input is an expression (e.g., a program) in one language (the source language) and whose output is a corresponding expression in another language (the object language).
universal function	A function whose arguments are expressions representing any computable function and its arguments. The value of the universal function is the value of the computable function applied to its arguments.

Printed in the United States
By Bookmasters